Contemporary Design Africa

Contemporary
Design Africa

Tapiwa Matsinde

Thames & Hudson

'If you can envisage it,
you can accomplish it.
If you can imagine it,
you can reach the heavens.'

Zimbabwean proverb

**Dedicated to the designers,
makers and artisans of Africa;
and to my Father**

First published in the United Kingdom
in 2015 by Thames & Hudson Ltd,
181A High Holborn, London WC1V 7QX

Contemporary Design Africa
© 2015 Tapiwa Matsinde

British Library Cataloguing-in-Publication Data
A catalogue record for this book is available
from the British Library

ISBN 978-0-500-29162-7

Printed and bound in China by Shanghai
Offset Printing Products Limited

To find out about all our publications, please
visit www.thamesandhudson.com.
There you can subscribe to our e-newsletter,
browse or download our current catalogue,
and buy any titles that are in print.

Page 1: Tekura, tables and stool on table;
Diallo Design, Dibi chair; Ronél Jordaan,
porcupine cushion and boulder cushion;
Mud Studio, chandelier; ZENZULU™, wire
lace platter on table. Ceramics, from
left to right: Louise Gelderblom, white
earthenware pleated vessel; Katherine
Glenday, white porcelain vessels with indigo
glaze; Astrid Dahl, white earthenware vessel;
Gone Rural, hand-woven grass table runner
with recycled plastic sequins (draped over
the Tekura bench).

Page 2: Dar Leone, Tropic Marine
collection, Dea Hots floor cushions (detail).

Page 3: Moroso, M'Afrique collection,
2009; Nopolou chair by Birsel + Seck.

This page: Beaded vases on stairs,
Safari Fusion.

Contents

Introduction / 6

Design Africa / 8

Africa's Creative Skills / 16

Design Showcase / 22

Basketry / 24 · Ceramics / 42
Furniture / 60 · Lighting & Decor / 112
Textiles / 140

Glossary / 202 · Map / 203
Further Reading & Resources / 204
Index / 205 · Picture Credits / 208
Acknowledgments / 208

'Design is becoming more eclectic...design increasingly reflects the cultural diversity both of its established Western markets and expanding ones in Asia, Africa and Latin America, where a new generation of designers is emerging. Those designers are defining their own approaches, which are influencing their peers elsewhere.'

Alice Rawsthorn (nytimes.com)

Introduction

Opposite: Zenzulu™, cone vessel.

In a 2009 TEDGlobal talk, acclaimed Nigerian author Chimamanda Ngozi Adichie spoke of the danger of 'the single story': how if we repeatedly see or hear only one narrative about a person or place, we risk 'harbouring a critical misunderstanding'.

Frequently mistaken for a country, and far more often the subject of negative than of positive news reports, the African continent has become a prime example of the effect 'the single story' can have on shaping perceptions. What happens in one region or country (particularly if it is something frightening or bad) is assumed to apply to the whole. This is despite the continent being a place where countless intricately layered stories abound – of good and bad, wisdom and warnings, joy and sorrow – all of them tightly woven into the very fabric of society.

For far too long, design and creativity from Africa have also been defined by a 'single story'. Perceptions of Africa's design have been shaped by romanticized views of an untamed continent shrouded in mystery and wonder. Imagery such as wooden statues, masks, animal prints, tribal markings, safari chic, ebony and ivory, and earth tones is assumed to sum up the aesthetic of an entire continent. In reality, the creative output of Africa has long been hugely diverse, shaped by multiple layers of culture and tradition, colonial legacies, and migrations from villages to cities to entirely new countries. It cannot be represented by a single aesthetic.

From recognizable heritage influences to abstract renderings, Africa's design today is a vibrant collection of individual expressions translated into compelling visual narratives that are making a mark on the global design industry. In the process, they reflect a creative African landscape that is full of possibilities; designers and makers are beginning to take advantage of these possibilities. From art and design to fashion and music, a creative reawakening is happening – a reawakening that is long overdue, given the continent's acknowledged influence on Modernism in Western visual art, and ongoing contribution to global creative inspirations. Yet despite this, Africa's designers themselves, with a handful of exceptions, remain almost invisible on the international stage.

This is changing, however, as design inspired by the continent is finally starting to shed the stereotypical connotations that surround it, and showing itself to be so much more. To continue to label design produced or inspired by Africa as 'primitive', 'tribal' and 'exotic' – fickle caricatures that fade in and out of style – is to do its creators a disservice. A generation of Africa's designers are translating their view of Africa's design into beautifully crafted products, and creating an aesthetic that is as diverse as the countries and cultures that make up the continent.

With a primary focus on interiors, this not entirely exhaustive book brings together the work of outstanding designers, makers and organizations based on the continent and beyond, whose work captures the sophistication, vitality, diversity and soulfulness that are shaping the African identities of the 21st century.

'The African continent is extraordinarily rich in creativity, materials and ideas that are sources of inspiration and nourishment for us. When applied to design, they engender products which exude tradition and modernity, innovation and history, form and beauty.'

Patrizia Moroso

Design Africa: From Past to Present

Africa's design foundations are rooted in a culturally rich and artistic past: one that has produced some of the world's most iconic objects and artforms, many representing the timelessness and ingenuity of the classical designs. These designs are continually referenced in much of the continent's contemporary creative output. Going beyond the realm of Africa's designers, the continent's rich creative traditions are a seemingly endless source of ideas across the world; countless captivated designers have drawn inspiration from the continent for decades, adapting and fusing their findings into their designs. And just as the continent's creative heritage has influenced and inspired designers across the globe, so too have Africa's designers been inspired by external influences, absorbing and relaying other traditions back through their work.

Design Past

Once revered in ancient kingdoms where master artisans were granted special status, the creation of visual art was an integral part of Africa's societies. The term 'visual art' refers to such disciplines as ceramics, textiles and carving. Artisans were adept at achieving beauty in the harmony of colour, pattern and form, while retaining the required functionality. Visual arts had specific meanings and objects were created to fulfil personal, domestic or ceremonial needs, as opposed to generating incomes; or, as noted by art history scholar Susan Vogel, with trade, galleries and museums in mind. The commercial value of Africa's visual art is widely thought to have begun with the flourishing of international trade, when products adapted specifically for external markets began to emerge.

Trade, and later colonialism, had a profound effect on the way Africa's visual art has been viewed, occurring first with Portuguese traders in the late 15th century, then Arabs in the 18th and 19th centuries, and Europeans around the mid-19th century. While it may appear that Africa's ancient visual art has been well documented, and subject to much research into understanding significance, symbolism, role and purpose, this is not entirely the case. Carried out from a Western perspective, documentation often incorporated the personal tastes of the collector, an approach that inevitably came with a range of inaccuracies and misunderstandings: the debate is ongoing.

The term 'design' as a discipline was not seen to apply to aspects of Africa's classical visual art. While the emergence of a viable design industry may be recent, the element of design in Africa's creativity should not be seen as something new. What was created would have been well thought out, refined until fit for its intended purpose. The increasing interest in, and collection of, Africa's visual art coincided with great changes in Europe, where the industrial age was leading to preferences for the machine-made over the handmade. This development, as art historians John Picton and Janet B. Hess note, would, in turn, dictate classification of Africa's visual art, in that, 'artforms such as masks and sculpture would fit neatly into the category of fine art, whereas disciplines such as pottery and textiles would be seen as craftwork, a genre that was deemed to be lowlier than fine art.' When viewed from an African perspective, disciplines that hold craftwork in much higher esteem challenge these long-held beliefs, so giving Africa's visual art greater significance in global art and design.

Africa's visual art was generally divided into three key periods: pre-colonialism, colonialism and post-colonialism, with output from the pre-colonialist era being the most highly prized. Vogel notes that this was primarily because this was, and still is in some instances, thought to be the period when pure authentic forms of visual art were produced, largely untainted by external influences. This led to the assumption that any originality and inventiveness in Africa's visual art ended with the beginning of colonial influences: a belief that is being refuted by modern day curators, scholars and collectors. Visual art across the continent has always allowed for a high level of creativity and resourcefulness and, as African art curator Sidney Littlefield Kasfir underscores, to suggest otherwise would be to discount the fact that Africa's creativity has never stagnated, but continues to flourish because societies still produced, and continue to produce, visual art for practical use. Over the centuries factors including migration, nomadic lifestyles and differing cultural groups have all left their mark upon creativity in Africa, as adapting to new locales and ways of doing things were incorporated into existing traditions. It is also important to note the effects trade and colonialism have had on creativity in Africa. European, Indian and Islamic cultures have all been assimilated into various local cultures at different times, creating new expressions. One only has to look at East Africa, where Islamic influences are deep rooted in Swahili culture, while the further south you go the more prevalent Dutch and Scandinavian design sensibilities become, stemming respectively from the arrival of Dutch settlers on the Cape coast and architectural collaborations in the latter half of the twentieth century.

A lack of relevant, namely pre-colonial, examples also affected documentation. This can be attributed in part to work being rejected, lost or destroyed if it was deemed by the collector to be either of no great importance or too primitive or ritualistic. In areas where nomadic cultures such as the Maasai, Himba and Tuareg existed, it would have been harder to collect and document findings if their creations were habitually left behind when no longer needed. With more sedentary cultures such as in Central Africa and the Kingdom of Benin in West Africa, more examples would have been available. Once creations had reached end-of-life or outlived their usefulness they would

'Design exists in many forms, interpreted and valued differently by many cultures.'

Romuald Hazoumè, Benin artist
(African Masters)

be destroyed: broken apart to be re-formed into something new, or replaced with a completely different version. Objects were also hidden or buried, especially in the case of a deceased owner, while marriage would often see the creation of new pieces.

Another issue was that colonial collecting and documentation tended to attribute work to a tribe or region as opposed to an individual. The anonymity of an artist was seen to add mystery, and this, as Kasfir notes, enabled a general perception that one artist's work could represent an entire culture and continent, thereby facilitating the assumption that the whole culture was homogeneous. Post-colonial documentation started to recognize individual designers, artists and artisans. As Kasfir notes, this has resulted in individuals making a name for themselves – the Nala ceramics dynasty, textile artists Nike Davies-Okundaye, Papa Ibra Tall and the late master weaver Gilbert Ahiagble, master woodcarver Abel Zata and furniture artist Baay Xaaly Sene to name a few; all of their work has served to bridge the gap between the past and a present shedding its outdated opinions.

Design Present

Africa's contemporary designers are exhibiting a renewed confidence in defining their own views about what constitutes design; they are developing innovative approaches to creating sophisticated products, as well as showing a commitment to upholding a legacy of excellence in execution and craftsmanship. Catering to the needs of a growing African consumer base, design in Africa is an industry that is carving out its niche not only in a rapidly evolving continent, but also in the wider world as global competition calls for products with wider commercial appeal. Whether it be drawing directly from local heritage and culture, or taking inspiration from other design sensibilities unconnected to a perceived African aesthetic, design emerging from the continent is not about designers trying to create something that looks 'African', but rather the exploration of bringing fresh, imaginative and sometimes unexpected perspectives to what is deemed to be African design.

To use an all-encompassing label such as 'African design' when referring to design from the continent raises several complex issues around race, culture and identity. The ever-increasing dialogue about the development of Africa's design within individual countries of heritage, and across the wider continent, encompasses home-based talent, a global diaspora, and non-Africans who either work in the continent or have made it their home. Added to this are the varying states of existing design industries in the continent's culturally diverse countries. Africa's main design industries are currently concentrated in specific countries such as Morocco, Senegal and South Africa; each exhibits a distinctive homegrown style. And while the concept of design as part of Africa's creativity is not something new, the existence of design as a sustainable industry is. As Design Network Africa (DNA) curator Trevyn McGowan explains, 'that newness is the reason why we need to speak of "African design"; it's still in its infancy and it needs to be held by the concept of the continent.' So as design industries continue to develop, the emphasis should shift towards individual countries rather than continually referencing the continent as a whole.

The combination of 'global savviness with local flavour', as South African design magazine *VISI* puts it, is one of the key characteristics defining design across the continent. This also includes the reinvention or revival of creative traditions. Another characteristic is being inventive with available materials, responding to the needs of urban living and creating sustainable solutions to address social and environmental concerns that not only work locally but can also be adapted globally.

Sustainability by Design

In the 2000s 'recycling', 'upcycling', 'ethics' and 'sustainability' became buzz words in a Western society seeking solutions to moral issues ranging from child labour exploitation, to the amount of waste accumulating in the world and the detrimental effects of throwaway cultures. Across Africa, however, recycling and resourcefulness are a way of life, not a luxury but a necessity, based on an innate obligation not to waste what can potentially be reused. It is a direct consequence of how expensive it is for many simply to replace old or broken items with a new version, or for some designers and artisans to invest in new raw material. Found objects and reclaimed materials have been incorporated into Africa's visual art throughout the centuries and the continent's artisans, in particular, continue to exhibit remarkable ingenuity in finding a use for what has been discarded. As cities become increasingly populated, the question of how to deal with accumulating post-consumer waste blighting streets and cityscapes has become a real issue for many African countries. It may not always be visible in upmarket fashionable areas, but the stark contrast of slums and townships often tells a different story.

By being resourceful and using the materials they have to hand, some designers and makers such as Cheick Diallo, Ousmane Mbaye, Heath Nash and Hamed Ouattara have become advocates for change, taking the lead in employing thoughtful, intelligent design solutions that re-use and recycle anything from plastic bags to discarded tyres. This process of transforming rubbish into objects of beauty to be coveted has given rise to genuine engagement with sustainable and environmentally conscious production, and is positioning the continent at the forefront of the sector. Sustainable design is not just about the environment. Embracing wider social responsibility, the industry has become an important vehicle used to address other pressing social issues such as creating sustainable design solutions for the betterment of communities and the world around them. In the words of Professor Mugendi K. M'Rithaa, an industrial designer, educator and researcher at the Cape Peninsula University of Technology Design, and a staunch supporter of inclusive, socially responsive and responsible design, 'It is about design for, and with, society. Solving problems with the input of local communities. Designers who ignore the plight of our local communities risk becoming irrelevant to their collective aspirations in the long run.'

Design for Change

The 'spirit of togetherness' is a sentiment that resonates through many African cultures, bringing people together for the benefit of the whole, and the same can be said for aspects of the continent's design industries. Consciously working towards real and lasting positive change and the upliftment of others, many of those featured in this book draw on the talents of those within their local communities and offer much-needed employment, training and exposure to better practice. For instance, prominent Malian furniture and product designer Cheick Diallo has made a commitment to share his knowledge, working with artisans, designers and studios across Africa.

Such collaborations facilitate the exchange of ideas, skills and techniques to make new and better products. At the same time, increased global interest and initiatives in areas such as ethics and fairtrade have also helped generate support and investment, bringing artisanal craftsmanship, in particular, to a wider audience. Cross-cultural collaboration with peers across the world becomes ever more accessible in an age of mobile digital communication. For instance, in Malawi, Maria Haralambidou of People of the Sun engages international designers and architects such as Rentaro Nishimura and Donna Wilson (for SCP) to design products that are produced in collaboration with the artisans supported by the organization. Recognizing the benefits of good design to showcase its high quality of craftsmanship and furniture manufacturing standards, Botswana-based Mabeo Furniture has strategically positioned itself to attract design-led collaborations with some of the world's leading designers. Founded in 1996 by Peter Mabeo, the award-winning company has worked with designers Patty Johnson, Patricia Urquiola and Garth Roberts, to name but three.

Other notable collaborators include American industrial designer Stephen Burks. His commitment to sustainable design and interest in connecting cultures and classical craft techniques from around the world with contemporary aesthetics has included the development of ingenious designs that celebrate Africa's basket-weaving traditions. As part of his Man Made project, Burks collaborated with basket-weavers

from Senegal and has also worked with other designers and artisans through DNA and Aid to Artisans programmes, including wire furniture designer Willard Musarurwa. French designer Sandrine Dole, who uses design to aid social and sustainable development, has mainly worked in West Africa, and since 2006 has made Morocco her home, where she works with local artisans. Patrizia Moroso, creative director of the Italian design house Moroso, invited leading designers Ayse Birsel and Bibi Seck, and Patricia Urquiola and Tord Boontje to design a range of furniture in collaboration with the artisanal workshop she set up in Senegal, recycling the traditional fishing nets used by local fishermen. The original designs were presented as part of the *Moroso M'Afrique* exhibition in 2009.

Promoting Design

Power shortages, logistical inefficiency, inadequate infrastructure and access to markets are some of the key challenges currently affecting just some of Africa's design industries. Helping designers and makers to realize their potential for commercial success and providing much-needed platforms for exposure is a priority. To this end, the past decade and a half has seen the emergence of local and international organizations and exhibitions, dedicated to developing and promoting the creativity coming out of, and inspired by, the continent. The ensuing partnerships ranging from business mentoring to product development have enabled designers and makers to connect with their peers, and showcase work to wider audiences through trade shows and exhibitions.

Organizations in the sector include the Network of African Designers (NAD), formed in 1999 as a platform for designers on the continent to exchange best practices, the South African-based Design Network Africa (DNA) funded by the Danish Centre for Culture and Development, and the US-based Aid to Artisans. Source, an agency promoting South African design internationally, was founded by DNA curators Trevyn and Julian McGowan, and brings selected products to big name retailers such as The Conran Shop, West Elm, Bergdorf Goodman and Anthropologie. In 2007, Arterial Network, a dynamic Pan-African network of artists, cultural activists, NGOs and creative sector individuals and organizations, was formed. Arterial Network organizes the African Creative Economy Conference, an annual platform for examining the potential problems and solutions in building a sustainable African creative economy.

Over the years a number of landmark exhibitions have introduced Africa's contemporary design to new audiences. In 2004, *Design Made in Africa* was an international touring exhibition featuring contemporary design by 30 designers from 14 African countries. The exhibition was an initiative of the Association Française d'Action Artistique (AFAA), Saint-Etienne Métropole for the SIAO (International Arts and Crafts Fair in Ouagadougou, Burkina Faso) and the Saint-Etienne International Design Biennial. *New Africa* opened at the 2007 INDEX Awards in Copenhagen and saw 45 designers from 13 countries addressing issues such as cultural strength and identity, empowerment, sustainability and the improvement of living conditions through design. *Africa Now*, part of the World Bank's Art programme, ran from 2007 to 2008 and featured contemporary art, design, fashion, film and photography from across the continent. Between November 2010 and May 2011 an unprecedented exhibition challenging the presumptions of what constitutes an 'African' style or aesthetic brought together the work of designers, artisans and architects of African descent in the Museum of Arts and Design, New York's *The Global Africa Project* curated by Lowery Stokes Sims. As South Africa became the first African nation to host the World Cup in 2010, the *Pan African Craft Exhibition* (PACE) was held in Johannesburg. Curated by Adam Levin and Andile Magengelele, PACE showcased cutting-edge craft and design from African designers and makers and was intended to challenge conventions and stereotypes.

As part of London Design Festival 2013, the exhibition *Graphic Africa* unveiled the work of Design Network Africa (DNA) members and a month later, in October, the opening of the Museum of African Design (MOAD) in Johannesburg saw the institution claim the title of being Africa's first museum dedicated to promoting design from across the continent. In 2014, Design Indaba, South Africa's seminal annual design conference and expo, celebrated 20 successful years of incubating and championing South African design, and marked a shift in focus as it expanded the format to embrace creativity from across the continent in the *Africa is Now* exhibition. Also in 2014, the inaugural Africa Design Award was held in Gabon as part of the prestigious New York Forum Africa conference. Founded by award-winning Moroccan interior architect and industrial designer Hicham Lahlou, the award is a visionary initiative to celebrate and fly the flag for contemporary design and innovation across the continent in all its forms.

Investing in the Future

To keep the momentum going and create truly sustainable design industries there is still much to be done. To aid development, greater support and investment are needed, both from governments and from the private sector. In many African countries, a creative economy still has to prove its economic worth alongside the main economic sectors such as agriculture, mining and tourism. Also, designers and makers in Africa more often than not face local markets that are not fully receptive to what is made locally by a local designer: this is for various reasons, including perceptions of quality, cost and the desirability of foreign brands. This situation has seen several successful African designers cite the need to build a reputation internationally before achieving acceptance at home. That said, attitudes are changing and there is growing interest in buying local, but, as designer Bibi Seck points out, it is more expensive so usually only those with money can afford to do this. However, as populations get wealthier, and, crucially, more design-aware, the demand for and investment in more sophisticated products and services will increase. There is also a need for increased investment in design education, creating the types of institutions that nurture the designers of the future, teaching them not only the fundamentals of design but also how to create the kind of design Africa, and indeed the world, needs. As Seck underscores, '[Design] education is very important. People who are making the decisions at the top need to understand the role of design in the development of the country.'

Design schools also need to find ways of preserving artisanal approaches to design and problem solving, as it is also important for designers to recognize the ongoing role of craft cultures in design: as textile artist Aboubakar Fofana notes, 'the craft element is the beginning of design.' And part of what makes design from Africa so compelling are the stories woven into the forms, moulded into clay, etched onto surfaces: seeping into the very heart of the products created.

Crafted by Design

Intertwined with the development and expression of design in Africa, the hand-crafted approach of the master craftsperson, be they designer–maker or artisan, occupies a significant role. It is one that sees the creative skills and ingenuity of roadside artisans, small-scale artisanal groups and individuals engaged to provide the level of skill and craftsmanship that designers seek to realize their designs, and collaborating to devise new production processes. Implicit in the term craft is not only the dictionary definition – the skilful making of decorative or practical objects by hand – but also the historical heft of inherited cultural traditions. And craft – incorporating classical craft – brings a soulfulness to Africa s design that is hard to ignore.

The strengths of the continent's classical craft heritages lie in the exceptional quality of artisanal handiwork, the ability to render exquisite detailing through skills that are difficult to replicate by machine and the sense of exclusivity that comes from no two products being exactly the same. However, pressure to meet commercial demands means the hand-crafted nature of craftwork has come under increasing threat from mass production, compromising creativity, individuality and quality. While some embrace the change, others, such as furniture designer Joëlle le Bussy, are attempting to resist industrialized production processes in their workshops, preferring to use traditional techniques.

Rejuvenating Classical Crafts

It seems that the more globalized the world gets, the greater the interest in, and revival of, local handicraft traditions. According to the Luxury Society, this shift has brought with it a growing emphasis towards 'authenticity in production, and valuing what has been made by hand'. For African countries, as with many the world over, migration to cities and the ensuing rise of urban living has seen the demand for a country's traditional products fall away, often in favour of imported goods, which are usually deemed to be better. This decrease in demand has led to a reliance among talented artisans on making and selling their wares specifically for the tourist market.

Along the roadsides of many African cities and towns the abundance of art and craft is unavoidable: the result of products copied and reproduced to the point of exhaustion because this is what sells – and, for most, is a much-needed source of livelihood. While this is a scenario replicated in many tourist-dependent destinations across the world, for the African continent global under-representation of work by Africa's designers means that these works usually end up representing a generalized view of African design. While helping to elevate the status of crafts beyond the humble craft stall, design from Africa should not be confused with art and crafts made for the tourist market, the rise of which occurred at the same time as Africa's classical art was having a profound effect on European artists of the early twentieth century, notably Pablo Picasso, Henri Matisse and their contemporaries.

Unsurprisingly, decline in demand has subsequently led to some local skills dying out and the loss of crucial knowledge that would traditionally have been passed down from mother to daughter, father to son. Each successive generation would refine the tried and tested designs and techniques and, as the process evolved, tell the stories of the new generations. However, when one generation loses interest, the chain is broken, in some cases lost forever in the memories of those who have passed, and sadly this has been the case with many of the continent's undocumented creative skills.

That said, efforts are being made to reverse this trend, and in some cases to pick up from where the chain left off. Far from being constrained by their cultures, designers across the continent and beyond are continually tapping into their heritage in search of inspiration, and a respect for both the old and the new has resulted in some of the continent's most innovative design and artisan talent working together

'Craft imbues the spirit of excellence which distinguishes good design from mediocre.'

Mugendi K. M'Rithaa

to modernize classical crafts. Learning from each other and experimenting, they breathe new life into the techniques of old, adapting the past to change through the use of new materials or novel applications of the old ones. Diversifying from the parameters of cultural and traditional use, sophisticated and imaginative approaches to craftwork have resulted in the blurring of boundaries between ancient craft and contemporary design aesthetics, as seen with renowned textile designers Aïssa Dione and Mariem Besbes, indigo dye master Aboubakar Fofana and South African designer Haldane Martin's innovative use of classical Zulu weaving into modern furniture designs.

And by incorporating classical crafts designers have become keepers of the past, helping to preserve the creative traditions of the past by recording them in the designs they are influencing in the present, for the benefit of the future.

Africa's Creative Skills

Africa's diverse and enduring, creative and cultural artforms showcase skills that have survived the centuries. Basketry, ceramics, metalwork, woodcarving and weaving and textiles were, and still remain, the most prevalent disciplines. Basic forms of each unite much of the continent, with differences according to region, tribe or culture occurring in techniques, depictions and decoration. Works would often be embellished with made and found objects such as beads, seeds, natural fibres (for instance, raffia), shells, embroidered textiles, leather, ivory and bits of metal. The more elaborately adorned or carved an object, the greater the cultural significance or standing of the owner.

Basketry

Found throughout many regions in Africa, basket-weaving saw skilful hands weave strands of natural, locally harvested materials such as wild grasses, small vines, palm leaves, bamboo and papyrus into strong, sturdy objects, usually containers and bowls. The Zulu ukhamba, Rwandan agaseke, Ethiopian mesob, Tonga bowl and Ghanaian Bolgatanga were just some of the highly functional objects created for winnowing, serving food, carrying liquids, and as storage for grains and clothing. Typically characterized by a diverse range of intricate patterns, woven baskets are like fingerprints: they bear the creative hallmarks of the weaver, the subtle variations rendering each one slightly different from any other.

Ceramics

Ceramics are said to represent one of the continent's oldest artforms, thought to date back to 9,400 BC based on fragments found in Ounjougou, central Mali. Widely practised across most of the continent, ceramics was a predominately female profession, although there are notable exceptions such as in North Africa where men took on the role. Ceramicists often lived at the edge of the village, close to the river banks from which they sourced their clay. The making of ceramics was limited to certain times of year, namely the dry season when the clay could dry more quickly. Expertly moulded by hand, or with the aid of simple tools such as stone shards and sticks, forms were adapted to suit a wide variety of functions; for example, pots with slightly elongated bases were designed to enable them to sit upright in the earth without tipping over. The level of skill was such that pots were more often than not perfectly symmetrical to the eye. In terms of decoration, items such as grass, seeds, corncobs, wood and shells would be used to embellish surfaces, in addition to stamping, incising and adding colour with slips.

Metalwork

Metalwork is thought to have emerged from the ceramics process of firing clay and interestingly as a profession dominated by men, historians note many of them were married to ceramicists. Metalwork led to the creation of objects such as agricultural tools, sculpture, currency and weapons. Metals were also inlaid into carved wooden objects including masks, bowls and stools. The most commonly used materials were iron, brass, bronze, copper and the rarer precious metals, silver and gold. Gold deposits and iron ore were found across parts of the continent, while copper was more plentiful in Central and Southern Africa.

The metalworking techniques employed included smelting, forging, hammering; and the lost wax method, which allowed for the production of hollow objects. Famous examples of metalwork include the Benin Bronzes, actually made using brass, once a rare and expensive alloy; and Asante goldweights, which were miniature carvings in copper, brass or bronze, used to weigh gold dust and at one time as currency.

Silver was more commonly used in North Africa, but due to rarity and cost, alloys, melted coins and found metal objects were used

as alternatives. North African artisans specialized in the art of filigree, which was introduced to North Africa by Jewish gold- and silversmiths settling in the region following the Spanish Inquisition in the 15th century. North Africa also saw the practice of hammered metal and punctured metalwork, a painstaking process of hand-punching tiny holes using a hammer and a punch, which was used in the region for thousands of years.

Woodcarving

Deeply ingrained in many African cultures, woodcarving was another skill carried out by men, and is noted for being either practised by nearly every man within a society or the domain of a select group of specialists. For some, as in the Casamance region to the south of Senegal, wood is an integral part of daily life: it is considered sacred, with carpenters said to pray over certain species before working on them.

Although other materials such as ivory, metal and stone would have been employed, wood was the most widely used material. Its use is attributed to the fact that it was relatively pliable; and as a readily available natural resource it helped to form a connection to the earth. Depending on the purpose of the object, geometric shapes, human forms, nature and other forms of symbolism, often intricate in detail, would be incorporated. Works were often carved out of a single block of wood and the finished piece was then polished, stained and decorated accordingly. Alongside sculpture and masks, seating is one of the most important and iconic genres in classical African carving. It was produced in various guises in the form of stools, headrests, backrests and thrones for personal or ceremonial use. In many ancient African societies seating was seen as a symbol of leadership and prestige, denoting the owner's wealth or status within the society. The European-style chair, whose adoption can be traced back to contact with the Portuguese, became a highly decorated object.

Textiles

Africa has a rich textile and weaving history, one that is tightly woven into the continent's diverse cultures and traditions. Historians note textiles have long been used as a commodity, a form of visual expression, a signifier of wealth, status and prestige or a sign of belonging to a specific group, for instance, family, as a means of marking special events such as the birth of a child, and documenting important religious, historical, political or social information. African art curator and author Christopher Spring observes how cloth connected the continent and helps trace the movements and migrations of people, highlighting how Trans-Saharan trade over the centuries saw North African textile influences reach Mozambique, where pieces with similarities to Berber textiles can found, while West Africans were inspired by North African patterns. Most prominent in North and West Africa, as John Gillow observes, the continent's textile traditions mainly constituted the weaving of cloths using hand-spun locally grown cotton and the dyeing and decoration of pre-woven cloths using techniques such as appliqué, embroidery and beading, a technique highly utilized in East, Southern and parts of West and Central Africa.

Weaving

Weaving was a predominately male profession, although women were involved in the spinning of yarns and decorative aspects. There were, however, exceptions – the Berbers of North Africa, for example. Weaving was done on hand-operated looms. A common technique saw the weaving of long narrow strips, which were then hand sewn together along the edges to make a wider fabric of contrasting patterns. Strip-weaving was a skill particular to the Asante and Ewe of West Africa, known for producing Kente cloth. The technique was also used by weavers in Liberia and Sierra Leone, making what is known locally as Country cloth, while the Yoruba of Nigeria produced Aso oke. In East Africa, Ethiopia had a reputation for being the 'cradle of cotton', its cotton weaving traditions said to date back to the reign of Queen Sheba, between 1005 and 995 BC, when woven cloths were traded. The Dorze and Konso peoples are renowned for their skills in producing the finest woven textiles.

Weavers would employ ingenious approaches to obtaining new threads. Hess notes how 17th-century Asante weavers began unravelling traded imported silk cloths and reweaving the threads into their designs. Locally sourced wild silk was used for prestigious cloths in West Africa, urban North Africa, Ethiopia and Madagascar. In rural North Africa and parts of West Africa, sheep's wool was used. Berber women traditionally wove flatweave tapestries and rugs, producing the styles *kilim*, which was woven, and *mergoum*, which was woven and embroidered.

Dyeing

Fabric-dyeing techniques ranged from tie-dye to indigo, using natural dyes obtained from local vegetables, plants and minerals. Over time, the use of synthetic dyes, which offered, among other things, a wider colour palette became more prevalent. In West Africa indigo dyeing was, and remains, one of the main cloth dyeing methods. Resist-dyeing was a popular technique, involving the tying or stitching of designs onto the fabric before dipping into dye. Tie-dye techniques were used in the Gambia, Côte d'Ivoire, Mali, Mauritania, Morocco and South Tunisia. Stencilling or painting solutions such as starch directly onto the fabric was another form of resist-dyeing: the Yoruba used a cassava root paste, in Senegal a rice paste was used and in Mali fermented mud, producing *bògòlanfini* or mud cloth as it is more commonly known. This last technique was pioneered by the Bamana women of Mali. In Zimbabwe, the country's dietary staple, *sadza*, has been used in recent times. The use of wax as a resist material was thought to have begun with the introduction of Javanese wax cloths by European traders.

Alternative Cloths

Thread was just one form of material used. In East and Southern Africa where woven cloth was not extensively produced, skins were more common. Uganda saw the creation of bark cloth, a centuries-old craft developed by the Baganda people of the ancient Kingdom of Buganda, who, as noted by Spring, reserved the wearing of certain types of decorated bark cloths for the *kabaka* (king) and royal family. Bark cloth is created from the bark of the tropical fig tree and is considered to be the oldest man-made textile. It was declared a World Heritage Material in 2005 by UNESCO. It is a natural, sustainable fibre as the bark regrows as long as the tree is stripped only once a year. Similarly, artisans in Chimanimani, the Eastern Highlands of Zimbabwe, produce *gudza*, a textile made by pulping, twisting, dyeing and then weaving fibres taken from a tree's inner bark.

Raffia fibres were used in Central Africa in particular, as well in the Congo region and in Madagascar. The best examples of raffia textiles are the complex geometric patterns of the Kasai velvet cloth from the Democratic Republic of Congo. Also known as Kuba cloth or simply velvets, these textiles were woven by the Shoowa people of the Kingdom of Kuba. The influences of Kuba cloth can also be seen in Namibia and Botswana, where it is known as *mashamba*.

Decorative Details

Africa's textiles employed many methods of decoration. Beading, appliqué and embroidery were popular techniques and often played a role in identifying peoples and cultures through the use of specific colours and patterns. Beads have been used in Africa for thousands of years, with some of the world's oldest examples being drilled ostrich shells dating back between 280,000 and 45,000 years. Ostrich-shell beads are still used, notably by the Himba people of Namibia. Other beads used included shell, bone, wood, ivory, seeds, horn, ceramics, glass, metal, and precious and semi-precious stones. Beading was practised in parts of West Africa and in East and Southern Africa, where beading traditions, most notably that of the Maasai, Ndebele, Xhosa, Zulu and Basotho, have long been admired for the intricate level of detailing in patterns and colours displayed, which were often more than decoration, but laden with meaning and conveying personal messages. Traders also brought with them a variety of glass beads, including Venetian Millefiori beads and brightly coloured glass seed beads, which were soon incorporated into designs, stitched onto cloths and leather hides.

Embroidery was practised throughout Africa. Several notable traditions include that of the Hausa women of Northern Nigeria, who are renowned for their

Below: Strip-weaving from Burkina Faso, originally part of the *Stripcloth Splendours: Contemporary Revival of West Africa's Textile Heritage* exhibition, 100% Design, 2013. Centre: *Bògòlanfini* cloth, Snob. Bottom: Kasai velvet cloth.

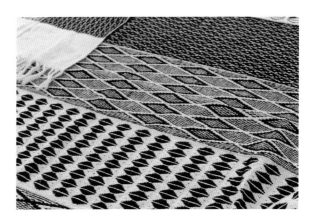

intricate hand-embroidery techniques, and the Shoowa, who carried out intricate embroidery and appliqué on their raffia cloths. In Ethiopia, delicate goldwork and metal-thread embroidery were two of the main embroidery traditions among the Amhara and Harar, and are still in use today. Once created using pure gold strands, often wrapped around silk, animal or human hair strands, goldwork is an ancient craft that can be traced back to Ancient Egypt, Babylon and Persia, its use and popularity having spread with travelling silk merchants. In North Africa, embroidery was inspired by the rich tapestry influences of Arabia and the Mediterranean. Appliqué was a particular skill of the Tentmakers of Cairo, an ancient craft passed down from father to son for generations, largely working in Cairo's Street of Tentmakers. The technique was traditionally used to decorate the interiors of majestic tent pavilions.

The European Cloths Made for Africa

Discussions about African textiles usually refer to wax cloth. Favoured across Africa, in particular West and Central regions, the bold vibrant prints of wax cloth fabric have for more than a century been synonymous with African dress and style. And as use of the distinctive fabric has grown in global popularity, it has inevitably made the transition into contemporary decor.

Although commonly referred to as African fabric or print by Africans and non-Africans alike, wax cloth is technically not an African fabric. The continent's association with the fabric, however, goes back many years. It was first imported in the 19th century via European traders and textile mills, who were seeking alternative markets for their wax-print batik fabrics, originally intended for the island of Java, which is now part of Indonesia. Finding the West and Central regions of Africa to be receptive and lucrative markets, British, French and Dutch companies vied for a share, most successfully the Dutch, for whom Java was a former colony known as the Dutch East Indies. Returnees from the island introduced the cloth and adapted production techniques to the Netherlands

and wider European markets. The Javanese patterns, however, did not appeal to the Europeans, leading to reproductions incorporating more European-inspired designs. As time progressed, African traders began requesting specific colours and designs, and as the fabrics grew in popularity the manufacturers themselves began adapting their designs to suit the tastes of their African customers, subsequently earning the fabric the title and recognition of being 'African fabric/print'.

Referred to as *ankara*, Java cloth, *lappa, pagne, capulana, kitenge* and *chitenge*, among other names, variations of the textile are now commonly found, firmly embedded in African dress and traditions. Although some African countries, notably Ghana and Malawi, produce their own local versions of wax cloth, Dutch *wax hollandais* is still seen to be superior. One of the leading manufacturers is the premium textile-manufacturing brand, Vlisco, a Dutch company that quickly established itself as a leader in a then-emerging market. Thanks to the brand's reputation for producing luxury, cutting-edge fabric collections, Vlisco's revered *wax hollandais* remains highly sought after by wealthy African consumers, as well as catering to a new generation of fashion-savvy Africans and designers across the globe.

Wax cloth was not the only European-made fabric to be adopted by Africa. In East Africa the brightly patterned *kanga* cloth reigns supreme. Also known as *leso*, the *kanga* is a distinctive cloth of social and political importance in East Africa, namely Kenya and Tanzania. The cloth is known locally for the Kiswahili inscriptions it bears, conveying lessons from words of wisdom to advice in areas such as health education. *Kangas* also signified wealth, measured by the quality and amount of cloth an owner had. Historians note how the fabric gets its name from *kanga*, Kiswahili for a guinea fowl, and is thought to have been given the name due to the prevalence of dots used in the fabric's earlier designs, which resembled the markings on the bird in question. There are several legends as to the origins of the *kanga*, the most popular pointing to printed kerchief squares called *leso*, which were brought to East Africa by Portuguese traders in the mid-19th century. A group of stylish women in Zanzibar are said to have bought the kerchiefs in lengths of six, cutting

> 'An image of "African fabric" isn't necessarily authentically [and wholly] African.'
>
> *Yinka Shonibare*

them into two lengths of three and then sewing them together along one side to make a three-by-two sheet, which they named *leso*. *Leso* was soon more popular than other available fabrics and local shopkeepers began ordering specially printed designs on a single unit of cloth, based on the stitched together pieces. Today, *kangas* are printed locally in Tanzania and Kenya.

Less well known is *shweshwe*, a patterned indigo cloth popular in South Africa, and produced locally in South Africa by Da Gama, a textile mill, which introduced brown and red versions. According to Da Gama's website, *shweshwe* is said to have been named after a local monarch, Moshoeshoe I, who was presented with the fabric as a gift by French missionaries in the 1840s. The gesture earned the fabric special status and the names *shoeshoe*, *isishweshwe* or *shweshwe*. The fabric was developed by European textile manufacturers in the 18th and 19th centuries and was manufactured in what was then Czechoslovakia (now the Czech Republic and Slovakia) and in Hungary by Gustav Deutsch, a local textile producer. When he relocated to the UK in the 1930s Deutsch brought the technique with him, setting up a factory in Lancashire. The fabric grew in popularity all over the UK with several other manufacturers taking up production. Exported to South Africa courtesy of the leading brand at the time, known as *Three Cats*, *shweshwe* was soon worn both by local Africans, who began wearing the cloth for traditional ceremonies, and the European settlers. The Germans, in particular, had a preference for the blue colour and the fabric's similarities to one they produced themselves called *blaudruk* or *blauwdruk*. *Shweshwe* has become a favourite of local designers.

Above from top: Vlisco fabric, Dutch wax block print, 100% cotton, Hommage à L'art collection; wax cloth, Super Ponex; Da Gama Textiles 100% cotton *Shweshwe* in sequin indigo; *kanga* cotton; Urafiki Tanzania printed *khanga* (Ftc Des No. 682).

Design
Showcase

Basketry

Africa's basket-weaving traditions have remained strong. In both urban and rural areas, baskets and other woven items such as mats are household staples, with many a street vendor ensuring a steady supply for both locals and tourists. Moving beyond its humble role in traditional African society to be recognized as beautifully designed artwork for display, basketry has become one of the finest examples of the merging of contemporary design aesthetics and traditional craft.

The classical styles are updated with modern shapes and vibrant colour palettes, which come from experimenting with dyes and modern materials. Alongside the traditional use of grasses, designers and artisans are also pioneering the adaptation of recyclable materials such as telephone wire and plastic, which offer greater flexibility in weaving more intricate designs. Modern basketry may also incorporate glass, metal and ceramics. Beyond traditional applications, basket-weaving techniques have been used in innovative furniture designs.

The basketry sector has great social impact. It employs mainly women, many of whom turn to the craft for a supplementary income, and it has been used as a means to unite people.

Madwa

Madagascar · Swaziland · South Africa

Madwa is a sustainable craft project that collaborates with small groups of master weavers in Madagascar, Swaziland and South Africa to produce contemporary woven homeware, accessories and textile collections.

> 'We believe in using the craft traditions and skills that exist and updating them with good product design to be relevant to an international market. We are committed to ensuring such skills and traditions survive.'
>
> *Kathy and Inca Waddell*

Madwa harnesses the unique weaving skills of the different cultural groups and regions where the company works and is inspired by craft and tradition: 'products that have an individual handprint and have been made using techniques passed down through the generations'. Contemporary colour schemes and patterns serve to modernize the traditional styles to create products that have been carried by the likes of Liberty and Tory Burch.

The company was founded in 2010 by South African mother and daughter team, Kathy and Inca Waddell, following a botanical tour to Madagascar. The duo were amazed at the wealth of craft skills found across the island, but were also very aware that a climate of endemic poverty throughout the country meant a limited scope for local artisans to use their skills to become financially independent and reach external audiences. They believed that with the right product development and support, a market could be developed to help sustain the artisans. This belief forms the company's core philosophy that the unique craft heritages should be preserved, developing quality products and providing a link to international markets. Madwa has since expanded the model to Swaziland and South Africa. In Swaziland, the company works with a group of women to make floor mats, using a local skill that had almost died out. The one master weaver left taught the women the technique and they are now working with Madwa to build a business that will sustain them and their communities.

Madagascar is home to diverse flora and fauna unique to the island, and over the years the environmental degradation has become a concern for many conservationists. For Madwa, this was another a key area to be addressed. From Madwa's conception they made a commitment to use only natural and sustainable materials such as raffia, palm and sisal, noting that 'protecting the natural environments protects the craft that originates from it'.

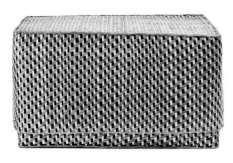

Tavie

Niger · The Netherlands

Tavie, meaning 'your life' in French, is a cross-cultural collaboration that brings together a dynamic group of Dutch creative professionals and almost 500 Tuareg women from Northern Niger to create a contemporary range of basketry centred on the Tuareg's rich artistic culture.

'A Tavie product is made with passion and pride, using the age-old traditional technique of palm-leaf weaving. Every Tavie product is unique, they are all hand-crafted to the highest quality.'

Cecile Meeuwsen

One of the last peoples still leading a nomadic life in Africa's central Saharan and Sahel regions, the Tuaregs' way of life is under increasing threat, and their strongly developed craft skills, such as palm-leaf weaving and silversmithing, make craftwork an important source of income.

Tavie was initiated in 2006 by Cecile Meeuwsen, founder of Tahoua Imports, a Sahelian company focused on handicraft development and promotion. Having witnessed the devastating effects of drought and hunger Niger experienced that year, Meeuwsen felt something had to change in order to help the communities she worked with to generate and maintain sustainable incomes. She coordinated a creative team, including graphic designer Edwin Everling and product designer Abke Geels of FLEX/the INNOVATIONLAB, to work with the Tuareg women and create design-led products that could compete in a global market. Geels spent several weeks in Niger developing the collection of baskets, bowls and platters: a valuable skill-sharing process for everyone.

Tavie's designs use the Tuaregs' different craft techniques to make one product. The bowls are hand-woven using the young leaves of the *doum* palm, a material respected by the Tuareg for its economic value. The leaves are combined with indigo dye, which has been used for generations by the Tuareg. The distinctive jewelry the Tuareg are renowned for is referenced in the form of silver discs placed at the heart of each bowl. Tuareg jewelry is often inscribed with intricate patterns, usually based on the Tifinagh alphabet. A silver metal tube bearing a unique number is incorporated into each Tavie product, which gives it a mark of authenticity. If a customer enters the number on the Tavie website they can find out more about its origin. The collection has been presented at some of Europe's leading exhibitions. However, since 2008 political instability in Niger's Northern region has hampered the development of this innovative basketry line.

Top: Tavie, Rayon de Soleil:
named after the decorated
silver disc in the heart of the
dish, which symbolizes the sun.

Above left: Tavie, Points du
Jour: the indigo markers
indicate the number of days
taken to complete the platter.

Above right: Tavie, detail
of the silver hallmark tube.

Right: Tavie, La Cascade:
the indigo block represents
a waterfall, which symbolizes
a haven of peace.

The New Basket Workshop

Zimbabwe · South Africa

The New Basket Workshop (TNBW) is a not-for-profit company that was founded in South Africa in 2008. Working predominantly with businesses run and owned by women, TNBW was built on a mission to rejuvenate and develop local basket-weaving industries, source viable markets and help improve the livelihoods of rural women across the continent.

'We believe in using the craft traditions and skills that exist and updating them with good product design to be relevant to an international market. We are committed to ensuring such skills and traditions survive.'

Frances Potter

Opposite: Tall porcupine basket developed by the weavers at the Lupane Women's Centre with design assistance from the New Basket Workshop, Snob.

Overleaf: Bamboo baskets made by bamboo weavers from Zimbabwe's Honde Valley with design input from India's National Institute of Design.

This mission is achieved through responding to market demands, by initiating design-led product development and innovative collaborations with the weavers. Under the guidance of co-founder Frances Potter, the organization has been particularly successful in Zimbabwe, where it sought to re-establish market links, which suffered under a period of economic and political instability, and forge new ones in the process. Funded by a grant from the Ford Foundation, TNBW assisted basket-weaving and craft associations in the south and west of Zimbabwe, including Binga Craft Centre, Zienzele Foundation, Bulawayo Home Industries and the Lupane Women's Centre as well as STEP Trust's Honde Valley bamboo weavers working in Zimbabwe's east, to create products that are sold by high-end retailers worldwide. Proceeds from the baskets sales are reinvested into the organizations themselves, with the decision on how and where to spend the money resting with the weavers and associations. Realizing the benefits that well-designed products have in a global marketplace, assistance with developing product-design skills is usually top of the list.

As a direct result of TNBW's work in Zimbabwe, 2010 saw the National Gallery of Zimbabwe host the critically acclaimed *Basket Case* exhibition sponsored by The Alliance Française, Zimbabwe. One of the results was a collaborative product development programme with Kingston University in the UK. Instrumental in raising the global profile of Zimbabwe's basket-weavers, TNBW has facilitated a five-country programme in Africa for India's National Institute of Design, aimed at improving the livelihood for women basket-weavers in Ethiopia, Ghana, Malawi, Zambia and Zimbabwe. In South Africa, TNBW is working together with the Africa Craft Trust, implementing a basket development craft programme in the iSimangaliso Wetlands of Northern KwaZulu-Natal.

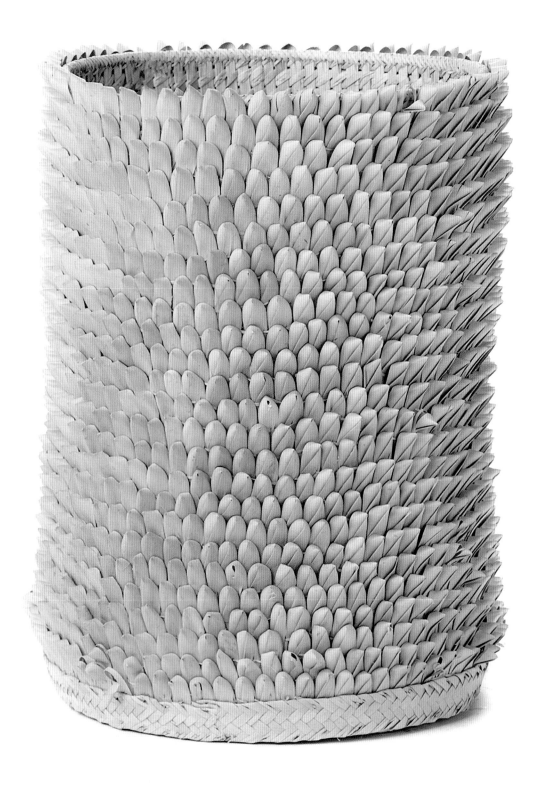

Tintsaba

Swaziland

'Tintsaba has made
it possible to raise and
educate my children.
It has given me a home,
security and a future.
It has taught me how
to work with love.'

Elizabeth Mngometulu

Meaning 'mountains' in SiSwati, Tintsaba is the name given to an award-winning company nestled high in the mountains of Piggs Peak, Swaziland. Tintsaba specializes in creating high-quality hand-woven products using sisal, a sustainable natural weed that grows plentifully in Swaziland.

Tintsaba was founded in 1985 by Sheila Freemantle, who, along with the traditional basket-weaving skills, was instrumental in bringing together basket-weaving groups and individual weavers in rural Swaziland. Tintsaba started with just a small group of weavers, who each began teaching others, drawing them into the Tintsaba family. Many of the weavers, such as Siphiwe Hlatswako, would have learnt basket-weaving from their mothers and other female elders, and through working with Tintsaba have honed their skills to reach the level of master weavers.

Tintsaba's baskets are graded according to technical skill. A basket can take up to 50 hours to complete. The production process is entirely by hand, from cleaning, dyeing and finely hand-spinning the sisals, to the distinctive hand-coiling techniques used. As the seemingly endless array of patterns have diversified from the traditional ones, dyeing the sisal with eco-friendly dyes has enabled more contemporary colour palettes. Tintsaba has trained over 890 weavers, buying the baskets they produce and selling them under the Tintsaba label. Tintsaba also works with international designers and technicians. Its commitment to excellence and design has earned the company recognition as the 'Master weavers of sisal in Africa'.

Tintsaba's much-loved founder passed away in 2012 and those she left behind are determined to continue her legacy. Many weavers such as Ester Mabuza and Thembi Dlamini are breadwinners, who supplement their income by basket-weaving. From inception, Tintsaba has been committed to individual development, supporting the weavers and a full-time staff of 15 with a continuous cycle of training, product development and business management skills, along with access to health and education facilities, including a mobile health clinic and a literacy training programme.

ZENZULU™

South Africa

'My aim is to engage with modernity by fusing traditions, techniques and technologies in my designs. Through ongoing innovation, and experimentation, yet remaining authentic and quintessentially African. I believe that human skill, invention and handwork infuses life into products.'

Marisa Fick-Jordaan

ZENZULU™ is a design-led craft business based in Durban, South Africa, that upholds eco-friendly and fairtrade practices. Known for its innovative use of telephone wire, ZENZULU™ resourcefully repurposes the material to create high-end, handmade decor products with bold patterns and mesmerizing colours.

ZENZULU™ was started in 1996 by South African designer and former political research fellow Marisa Fick-Jordaan, whose interest in transitional craft forms led to the formation of a local telephone wire-weaving project, mentoring a growing group of master weavers in using a coiled basket technique. As the possibilities of fusing traditional craft techniques with cutting-edge contemporary design aesthetics and modern industrial materials became evident, the project gradually expanded, teaching the new designs to unemployed women from both urban and rural areas. ZENZULU™ has since worked collaboratively with, and ensured sustainable incomes for, more than 150 home-based craft producers, the majority of whom are women.

Establishing ZENZULU™ was not without its challenges, most notably as there was only one basket mould to work with, limited material supply and design concepts that proved challenging to even the most skilful of weavers. Perseverance paid off as securing funding for skills development helped with sourcing a mould, while a wire manufacturer was 'coerced' into making fashionable colours to specification. The wire's copper core was replaced with mild steel to counteract rising copper prices that would have made production unsustainable. ZENZULU™'s products are regularly updated and manufactured to the highest quality standards. Continually working to redefine the possibilities of wire and basket-weaving, ZENZULU™ started to utilize the skills of Zulu master beaders: the combination of glass beads, wire and telephone wire leading to the expansion of the product range.

Sold around the world, ZENZULU™'s distinctively shaped vessels and sculptural pieces have become South African design classics, receiving numerous accolades and awards. The company has seen high profile

collaborations with the likes of Fabrica and fashion designer Oscar de la Renta. Fick-Jordaan also has a licensing agreement with Bosa Ceramics, Italy, to produce a platter entitled *Amasumpa*.

ZENZULU™'s work has been included in a number of international exhibitions, including *Design Made in Africa*, The Conran Shop's *Harare to Higgovale* exhibitions in London, New York, Paris and Tokyo, the cutting-edge exhibition *Design and the 21st Century* at the Holon Design Museum in Israel, and the 2010 Museum of Arts and Design, New York's ground-breaking *The Global Africa Project*. Fick-Jordaan has acted as a design consultant and product developer for craft development programmes across Africa, is a curator for the Design Indaba Expo and was a presenter at the 2007 TEDGlobal Africa Conference in Tanzania.

'By creating and maintaining a sustainable craft design business ourselves, we have helped to create hundreds of sustainable micro-enterprise craft businesses, through participation and mentoring.'

Marisa Fick-Jordaan

Left: Imiso Ceramics, hand-pinched tableware inspired by the richness of South Africa's flora.

Ceramics

Ceramics remain one of the staples of domestic rural life in Africa and as individual artists become recognized, traditional clay pots have been increasingly respected as collectables in their own right. The sector has produced a number of noted artists, such as the Nala family: three generations of female ceramicists from South Africa whose work takes the skill to new heights. Across the continent ceramics was a predominantly female profession, but as time has moved on, the discipline has seen more men taking up the craft, for instance, Nic Sithole, Clive Sithole and Bruno Sserunkuuma.

In towns and cities contemporary production and techniques have served to rejuvenate and keep the artform alive. Combining art with functionality, contemporary ceramicists are using clay as a canvas to explore wide-ranging themes from cross-cultural identity to the revival of forgotten traditions.

Imiso Ceramics

South Africa

Majolandile 'Andile' Dyalvane and Zizipho Poswa are the dynamic duo behind Imiso Ceramics, an innovative South African ceramics studio formed in 2006. Making a name for themselves in the world of contemporary ceramics and design, Dyalvane and Poswa draw inspiration from local tradition and nature to create products that combine their distinctive individual signature styles.

From whimsical pinched pots to sleek sculptural vessels, Imiso Ceramics' hand-crafted designs encompass functional ware and collector's items such as sculpture and tables, loosely grouped within themed collections. Meaning 'tomorrow' in Xhosa, the word *imiso* forms the basis of the company's slogan, 'Dawn of a new era', underpinning the hopes and dreams the owners have for themselves, the future and their flourishing business.

'The philosophy of what I do is atomic really, little splits and explosions of ideas, rhythms and history derived from my passion for clay and possibilities.'

Majolandile Dyalvane

'When I was a boy, in a little village called Ngobozana, Qoboqobo in the Eastern Cape... I had no idea that clay and design would transform my world,' says Dyalvane, recalling how his life changed when a village elder saw him sketching one day and suggested that he should go to a school that would help him to develop his skill. Dyalvane's brother, who worked to put him through a local training college, shared his view. Before founding Imiso Ceramics, Dyalvane worked at the Potters Shop, who sent him on a five-week exchange programme to Denmark with a number of other South African ceramicists. Here, his passion for ceramics was noted by a mentor and resulted in a scholarship to study at what is now Nelson Mandela Metropolitan University in the Eastern Cape. Graduating with honours in ceramic design, Dyalvane returned home to Cape Town to launch Imiso Ceramics, and this is where Dyalvane draws his greatest influences from: the landscapes, traditions, the Xhosa people, the artifacts and the music.

'Clay gives [me] the ability to create something beautiful, valuable and usable with the four elements of life: earth, water, air and fire.'

Majolandile Dyalvane

These influences can be seen in Dyalvane's work: from the incised marks that characterize the 'Scarified' collection, which evokes ancient African traditions of body scarification, to the everyday scenes from Imiso Ceramics' studio window, to the nod to Cubism in the 'Africasso' collection inspired by Pablo Picasso, who was himself influenced by African sculpture.

Poswa graduated in surface design, with a focus on textiles, from the Cape Peninsula University of Technology in 2003. Her love of textiles is constantly referenced in the textural patterns that adorn the clay in her work. Imiso Ceramics' hand-pinched ceramic collection, which was developed by Poswa, is popular with customers: the colourful whimsical style reflecting flowers in bloom.

Dyalvane and Poswa work from a studio gallery at the Old Biscuit Mill in Woodstock, Cape Town. From the beginning they chose to manufacture and sell their ceramics from the same studio space, attributing this practice to the success of the business, as visitors are able to watch the production processes, chat and interact with the artists at work, which helps to form a bond with the products they go on to purchase. Dyalvane and Poswa are committed to building a unique South African brand and have a strong determination to inspire other up-and-coming artists and entrepreneurs. Imiso Ceramics has exhibited internationally and is a member of Design Network Africa and Southern Guild.

Opposite: Imiso Ceramics,
table with ceramic elements.

Top left: Imiso Ceramics,
studio session.

Top right: Imiso Ceramics,
'Scarified' collection, slim
conical vase.

Right: Imiso Ceramics, 'Skyline'
collection, ceramic dinnerware.

Jade Folawiyo

Nigeria · UK

Combining traditional craft practices with contemporary aesthetics is an integral part of product designer Jade Folawiyo's work. The process allows her to explore the revival of old and the development of new techniques. Folawiyo works with ceramic, glass and metal, and draws inspiration from being a young Londoner of Yoruba heritage.

'I believe that objects have the ability to create meaning and a sense of belonging. It is for this reason that my work uses traditional techniques in a contemporary way. I enjoy learning about traditional crafts and using elements of cultural connection to give grounding to the pieces that I design.'

Jade Folawiyo

Intent on becoming a fine artist, Folawiyo's interest in art and fashion led her to enrol on a foundation course at Central Saint Martins in London, where she was drawn to product design, graduating with a BA in 2010. Folawiyo began designing her own pieces in the same year. From 2008 until 2009 she had a scholarship at Fabrica, where she worked with a team developing ceramic and glass collections for Secondome, an Italian gallery. The experience influenced her decision to specialize in luxury objects for the home.

Born and raised in London, Folawiyo spent childhood summer holidays in Lagos, encouraged by her parents to engage with Nigerian culture. Folawiyo continually references these experiences in her work; she believes that objects have the ability to create meaning and a sense of belonging, and for this reason she is always on the lookout for traditional techniques that are not being used in the mainstream. Folawiyo has collaborated with Venetian glass-blowers and Nigerian gourd-carvers, producing her 'Ile: Home Tableware' collection in 2013. Combining hand-carved, naturally grown calabash bowls from Nigeria's Oyo State with delftware-inspired ceramics produced in Kent, UK, the mix of materials and decorative elements creates an unexpected yet complementary aesthetic fusion between African and Western culture. The project also brings to light the calabash's properties as an entirely sustainable material: it uses very little energy to manufacture, and is biodegradable. Folawiyo hopes the project will help re-energize and preserve this forgotten tradition, while enabling the community to increase opportunities for export and revenue.

Another of Folawiyo's signature techniques is patinization: she has experimented with the colouring of metal, having noted how the technique had been used in arts and architecture across many different cultures for

Above and overleaf: Jade Folawiyo, 'Ile: Home Tableware' collection: the materials used are sourced from the area they represent. The gourds are hand-crafted in the village of Oyo in Nigeria, helping to re-energize a forgotten tradition, while the ceramics inspired by English delftware are produced in Kent, UK.

hundreds of years, but was largely neglected in design. She produced UNO, a range of copper lampshades, using patinization. She designed the range during a residency with the Design Museum, London, in 2011. The collection was part of a private exhibition for the Queen that celebrated 60 years of design in London. Following the Design Museum residency,

Folawiyo was invited to join the International Design Pool (ID Pool) designers in 2012 and worked on developing new product ranges for the widely acclaimed Portuguese porcelain factory, Vista Alegre. Folawiyo's work has also been featured in a number of International Design weeks.

'I love the way product design incorporates both drawing and creative thinking while enabling me to work on the breadth of projects available in this sector. I particularly enjoy working on pieces that adorn the home and creating functional pieces of art.'

Jade Folawiyo

Kpando

Ghana

The Volta region of Ghana, an area known for its skilled craftsmanship and distinctive ceramics, is home to Kpando, a business that was founded by ceramics designer Joseph Nii Noi Dowuona over a decade ago.

> 'Kpando pottery embodies essential elements which give life to evocative ceramic art.'
>
> *Amaridian*

Kpando's artisans create a range of decorative and functional interior ceramics such as pots, vases, water containers and platters. Dowuona works with 70 local women, creating the designs that they sculpt. Taking inspiration from ceramics that have been passed down through the generations, and giving them a contemporary update, Dowuona's designs are characterized by distinctive surface relief, etched patterns and perforations. Organic shapes with protruding knobbly bumps and spiky thorn-like shapes are reminiscent of gourds carved from the hard bulbous shells of fruit, while the tall slender forms call to mind cacti.

Kpando's ceramics are skilfully moulded by hand, without the aid of a potter's wheel, using a particular clay that is dug near Lake Volta, said to be the world's largest artificial lake. The clay is mixed with old broken pottery and water, hand-shaped and then further tapped into shape with the aid of wooden bats. After the firing process, the hot pottery is immediately placed into a pile of bamboo shavings instead of a clay oven: this finishing process produces a fire that gives the products their signature shiny black patina.

This finish has a metallic quality that belies the fragility of the clay and results in strong focal pieces. Kpando's ceramics have been stocked by a number of international retailers.

Below: Kpando, ceramic
cylinders, Amaridian.

Opposite: Kpando, ceramic pots,
Design Network Africa, 2013.

Mutapo

Zimbabwe

Mutapo, which means 'clay', is an innovative ceramics studio owned by ceramic artist Marjorie Wallace. Born in Bulawayo, Wallace attended the Michaelis School of Fine Art in Cape Town, graduating in fine arts with a major in painting. She returned to Zimbabwe shortly before the country became independent in 1980.

'When I started decorating pottery I thought more and more about baskets, how they look and how they are woven. They too are vessels. I saw my task as being no different from the basket-makers.'

Marjorie Wallace

Wallace was an art teacher for many years and taught at several government schools and at Harare Polytechnic. Her love of ceramic work led her to become an assistant to local ceramicist Ros Byrne, who gave her a solid grounding in the discipline; in 1992 Wallace took over Mutapo from the founders Howard Minnie and Maureen Morris.

Based in the Harare suburb of Hatfield, Mutapo mainly creates fine porcelain domestic ware collections. The Mutapo team is comprised of three members: Jairos Zangira, who does all the throwing and has been with Mutapo since the beginning; his son Basil, who recently started to make the clay and glazes; and Wallace, who decorates the ceramics. Wallace's designs are inspired by Zimbabwe's basket-making traditions which are familiar to her from her youth. The techniques she uses include scratching, pressing and incising to create linear designs and decoration.

Over the years, Wallace has opened the studio to other ceramicists and she also trains younger artisans. Artists who have worked with the team include Berry Bickle, Margie Fries, Kevin Hough and Bev Sterling. She has exhibited Mutapo's creations internationally and is a member of the pioneering Design Network Africa initiative. Mutapo exports much of its work to Europe and is experiencing increased demand from the Southern and East African regions.

Below: Mutapo, porcelain platter,
Design Network Africa, 2013.

Opposite: Mutapo, porcelain bowls,
Design Network Africa, 2013.

'Being African, and surrounded
by African things, inspires me.'

Marjorie Wallace

Left: Haldane Martin, Songololo sofa
at Phakalane, a retro-inspired sectional
sofa designed to curve into its location.
It is named after the millipede.

Furniture

Africa is renowned for creating iconic furniture pieces
such as the stool. Seating, in particular, has been an
important aspect of many African cultures and, in the
hands of the continent's contemporary designers, it
undergoes something of a metamorphosis, reinvented
and re-imagined as a continual source of inspiration.

Innovative approaches to furniture design and the materials
used redefine the way we interact with it. Aside from meeting
the needs of modern living, designs are also being used to
comment on issues such as sustainability, a common thread
linking designers and makers across all categories.

The expense of industrial manufacturing and raw materials forces
designers on the continent to seek alternative options, drawing on
the wealth of artisanal skills and making ingenious use of readily
available materials such as discarded wood, plastic and metals:
materials that inadvertently comment on our throwaway cultures.

Deeply rooted in the continent's enduring woodcarving
traditions, wood is reinterpreted into contemporary
heirloom-style pieces.

Artlantique
Senegal · Spain

'The real raw material is not only the actual wood from the boat, it is the life of the boat itself, that of its master and family.'

Ramón Llonch

Wood salvaged from old or discarded fishing boats is given a new lease of life as contemporary furniture, retaining the hallmarks of its former life. Along the coasts of West Africa, fishermen have long been a common sight, making daily trips into the Atlantic Ocean in brightly coloured narrow boats built by master craftsmen to withstand the daily demands of carrying the fishermen and their catch.

The boats are made from untreated Samba wood. Weathered by the elements, the faded illustrations and layers of peeling paint added over the boat's lifespan bring character and texture and in the process tell the stories of livelihoods, of the thousands of nautical miles spent riding the waves and of the people who carved them. It is this connection between fishing and carpentry that inspired the distinctive and colourful furniture of Artlantique.

Collaborating with a group of Senegalese carpenters and their apprentices, Spanish designer Ramón Llonch formed Artlantique in 2010, inspired by one of many trips through West Africa. Having spotted some abandoned boats while cycling through the Senegalese town of Saint-Louis, Llonch was immediately struck by 'the possibility of giving them another life', and made successive trips to Dakar to sound out the idea, which was well received by the local carpenters. Llonch, who studied arts and textile design in Barcelona and Italy and has worked as a design consultant in several countries, brought his skills to the role of coordinator of the project.

Transforming the boats, entirely designed and hand-crafted in Senegal, is an instinctive process, and Llonch wryly notes that the method 'to transform a fishing boat into a football table is not written in any book'. Boats that have passed their useful life but are still in good condition are bought from the

'The history of a livelihood: successes and failures. Our biggest challenge is keeping this story in the heart of each piece of furniture even after the process is completed. This is and will continue to be our aim.'

Ramón Llonch

fishermen and transported to the Artlantique workshop. Here the team remove the best pieces, deciding how to utilize the reclaimed wood most productively, taking into consideration the size of the boat, the tones of the wood and colour combinations, until a clear idea of the furniture piece emerges. No two boats are ever the same, making each piece of Artlantique furniture unique. Upon completion, the finished product is transported to Spain, where it is displayed.

Apart from ready-made collections, Artlantique also works to commission and has produced pieces for hotels, restaurants, retail shops, art galleries and contemporary design stores in Europe and USA.

'I'm proud to be part of a team and my wish is that in the future we have more people involved in this project, more voices, more talent.'

Ramón Llonch

Opposite: Artlantique, Taburet.

Below: Artlantique, Assane.

Birsel + Seck

Senegal · USA

In 2004, multi award-winning designers Ayse Birsel and Bibi Seck formed Birsel + Seck, a design studio that encompasses product design, fashion and interiors. Their clients have included Herman Miller, Target and Hewlett-Packard.

Birsel + Seck are problem solvers, creating products that adapt to a user's lifestyle needs: this is reflected in the principles of simplicity, empathy and sustainability that are at the core of their work. Talking about becoming a designer, Seck says 'I wasn't thinking of solving problems, I just wanted to draw!', but he soon realized that design brings with it a means of thinking of new solutions to the problems at hand. This is what inspires Seck: that a problem needs to be solved. He approaches his work with what he describes as 'the balance between emotion – the soul of the product – and rationality.'

Born in France to a Martiniquais mother and Senegalese father, Seck was raised in Belgium, London and Senegal, moving back to Paris to go to college. He originally planned to become an architect, but an interest in creating objects, such as furniture, boats, packaging and branding, led him to switch to graphic design with the intention of going back to work in Senegal. After graduation, Seck worked for Renault for 13 years, where he led the interior design teams for the compact SUV Scenic I and II, Twingo II and Trafic to create award-winning interiors. After meeting Birsel, Seck settled in New York, where Birsel had already established a successful design studio, Olive 1:1. Raised in Izmir, Turkey, Birsel came to New York on a Fulbright Scholarship to complete her Master's Degree at Pratt Institute.

Seck has fully maintained his connection with Senegal and in 2006 began working with local artisans. Describing his work in Senegal as being 'challenging, but more emotionally connected', Seck is a hands-on designer

> 'When I design I seek the balance between emotion – the soul of the product – and rationality.'
>
> *Bibi Seck*

'I wasn't thinking of solving problems, I just wanted to draw, but I soon realized that design brings with it a means to think of new solutions to the problems at hand... My inspiration is the user, the end user of the product I am supposed to design.'

Bibi Seck

Right: Birsel + Seck, the Taboo collection, comprising a table and stool, is inspired by the daily lifestyle of West Africans when dining and relaxing.

Opposite above: Birsel + Seck, Madame Dakar couch, M'Afrique collection, 2009.

Opposite below: Birsel + Seck, Bayekou, M'Afrique collection, 2009.

who seizes every opportunity to become fully immersed in a collaborative process with the artisans.

Birsel + Seck's projects in Senegal include working with Moroso on the 'M'Afrique' collection; Patrizia Moroso had established an artisanal workshop and invited them to create a 'Made in Senegal' collection. For Seck, the collaboration was a very different process from design development in the West, which he notes is often slowed down by the need to have meetings at each stage of the production process. Working directly with the artisans meant a much quicker process of moving back and forth from large-scale drawings to prototypes in quick succession, refining as they went along, until the final design was achieved.

Birsel + Seck also designed 'Taboo', an innovative range of furniture made from 75% recycled plastic bottles and rubbish bags, and produced by a local Senegalese company, Transtech, which manufactures water and septic tanks using recycled plastic and polyutherane. The collection came about when a friend, who was a painter, asked Seck to design a bench for an

exhibition. Seck created several designs in steel and was then introduced to Marie-Jo Sanchez, the owner of Transtech, and thought the company would be the ideal partners to produce the furniture. Seck began to explore plastic using the factory's auto-moulding capabilities and spent his time on the factory floor working with the team to experiment with the plastic and any other waste material he found. The colour of the furniture is dependent on the colour of the recycled plastic used.

Birsel and Seck have lectured widely, and served on the advisory panel for Design Indaba's 2014 *Africa is Now* exhibition.

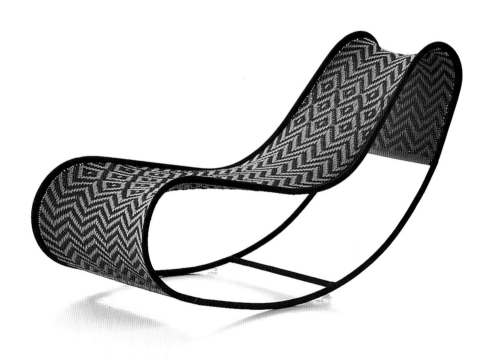

69

Diallo Design
Mali · France

'I was not interested in
just producing another
chair – I wanted to
look at another way
of sitting. I decided
to focus my design on
artisanal methods. With
the artisanal, one can
preserve the culture of
Africa and its savoir faire
and then elevate it and
make it contemporary
through design.'

*Cheick Diallo (Design Network
Africa, Guild Design Fair)*

**Cheick Diallo is one of the continent's leading furniture and product
designers and is recognized for his innovative and forward-thinking
designs that unite ancient traditions with contemporary aesthetics.
Diallo constantly pushes the boundaries of what defines design in Africa.**

The son of an architect, Diallo discovered a love for furniture design while
studying architecture himself at the Ecole Supérieure d'Architecture in
Rouen, France. He went on to study design further at the prestigious Paris-
based design school, ENSCI-Les Ateliers. After graduating, Diallo chose to
dedicate a large part of his career to pursuing opportunities in developing
the design industry across Africa rather than pursuing a design career solely
in France.

In 1997, Diallo opened his design studio, Diallo Design, in Bamako, Mali,
the country of his birth and has since developed a pioneering practice as
a designer, maker, producer, consultant and educator for design projects
involving an Africa-based development process. Diallo's practice extends
beyond the confines of his studio: from Bamako to Ouagadougou, the
streets of West Africa are his inspiration and he can often be found sitting
among the street artisans, interacting and watching how they develop
their designs as they go along, and tapping into the spontaneous creative
energy to inform his own design process. In tune with the artisans around
him, Diallo's iconic designs are created from materials salvaged from the
discarded debris of everyday life. Tyres, plastic, bottle tops, cans, scrap metal
and old fishing nets are transformed into elegant sculptural forms, whose
fluid lines are in keeping with his architectural background. Diallo also
incorporates many traditional techniques, working with local artisans such
as weavers, blacksmiths, jewellers, shoemakers, sculptors and ceramicists,
and in doing so actively promotes economic development in Mali.

Diallo has managed a large number of design workshops around the continent, helping businesses and artisans improve their products for export, both technically and stylistically. Diallo has also collaborated with other designers and design studios such as the Ghanaian-based furniture company, Tekura, and ceramic studio Kpando. In 1996, Diallo created the Association des Designers Africains (African Designers Association). Diallo has received several awards for his work and it has been widely exhibited throughout Africa, Europe, Asia and the US to critical acclaim. Diallo Design was part of the seminal exhibitions *Africa Remix* and *The Global Africa Project*, and Diallo is a regular guest at design biennials around the world.

'I do not have an interest in design if it is only to remake that which already exists.'

Cheick Diallo
(The Global Africa Project)

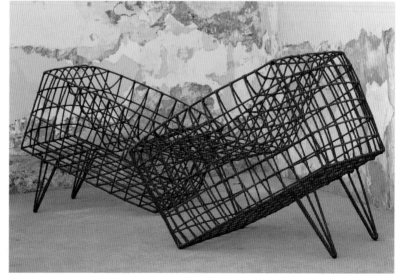

Dokter and Misses

South Africa

Launched in 2007, Dokter and Misses is the combined talents of married couple, industrial designer Adriaan Hugo and graphic designer Katy Taplin, who describe their work as 'modernist, with strong construction lines and bold colours that form graphic shapes and spaces'.

'The aim is to create work that is unique, high quality and functional; design that challenges, entertains and works. With humour.'

Katy Taplin

Working from a studio showroom in the Johannesburg suburb of Braamfontein, Hugo and Taplin produce an innovative selection of furniture, lighting and interior objects that have not only captured the imagination of South African interior design enthusiasts, but also that of international collectors. The couple, who met at university, very much inspire each other and attribute the growing success of their company to this. Hugo came to furniture design via sculpture at art school and went on to study industrial design at WITS Tech. Taplin studied information design at the University of Pretoria, working in various design fields including magazine editorial design.

Starting out with limited workshop space and no woodworking tools, Hugo and Taplin made use of what was available to them, adapting their processes as they went along. Initially using hand tools and silk screens, their work now employs a range of techniques, including laser-cutting and the use of bold graphic patterns and hand-painted surfaces, which have proven to be an important part of the Dokter and Misses aesthetic. Several designs feature contemporary reinterpretations of traditional African patterns. The geometry of Ndebele patterns are hinted at in the LALA Shwantla server, while their award-winning Kassena server combines art deco inspiration with the traditional patterns employed by the Kassena people of Burkina Faso to decorate the exterior of their homes. Dokter and Misses is a member of Design Network Africa and the pair have exhibited their work internationally.

74

'[Adriaan and Katy] are inspired by the idiosyncrasies of their surroundings, their modernist angular design has a bold upbeat energy that makes their objects and furniture immediately desirable and urban cool.'

Design Network Africa

Below: Dawn Dludlu for Dokter
and Misses, Hlambu table.

Bottom: Dokter and Misses,
LALA Shwantla server.

Opposite: Dokter and Misses,
Kassena server, heartbeat
lamp, sweat lamp and easy
mirror.

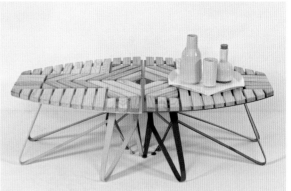

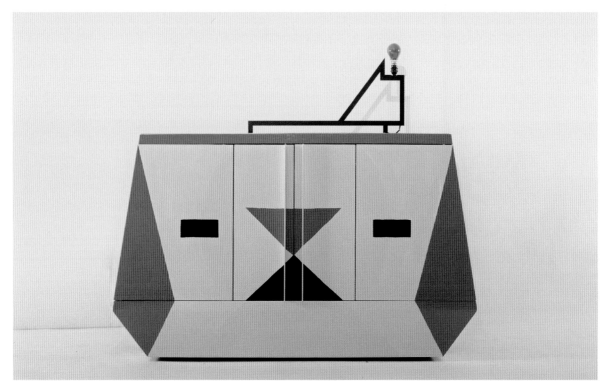

Feeling African

Zimbabwe · South Africa

Willard Musarurwa was born and educated in Zimbabwe and obtained a diploma in business studies. It was after he moved to South Africa in 2001 that he switched careers from business to furniture design.

'I think it is amazing for someone like myself, who comes from the township, to come up with a fantastic product that you can use, a high-end product.'

Willard Musarurwa

In South Africa, Musarurwa joined a network of artisans from Zimbabwe who were making crafts as a means of generating an income. But after five years of 'getting nowhere', Musarurwa wanted to push his skills to another level and in 2003 started his wire furniture crafting business, Feeling African. Musarurwa sought assistance from the Cape Craft and Design Institute (CCDI), a Cape Town-based craft business development organization; he credits them with helping him to develop as a designer-maker and expand his business. Having started out working from home in the township of Samora Machel, he moved to a spacious studio in Woodstock, home to many of Cape Town's creative businesses.

Musarurwa employs a small team of craftsmen who produce Feeling African's expertly hand-woven ranges of multipurpose all-weather furniture using powder-coated galvanized steel. The company caters to both a local and international clientele, and undertakes private commissions for architects, interior designers, retailers and private individuals. Musarurwa has also collaborated with leading designers, most notably with industrial designer Stephen Burks, through an Aid to Artisans programme. Burks was working with CCDI at the time Musarurwa joined. They worked together to create the TaTu collection for Artecnica. Featuring wire stools and tables, TaTu has become one of Feeling African's most successful products to date, appearing in a host of local and international media. Musarurwa also collaborated with South African interior designer Heidi Lise to adapt his Sallie design chair into a recliner, which Feeling African then produced. In recognition of the support received to build his business, Musarurwa has reached out to unemployed people in the township, offering training in crafts and encouraging them to explore opportunities to create their own businesses just as he did, saying, 'You don't only have to look for a job, you can create a job for yourself and other people.'

'I get a lot inspiration from the space that people have and are trying to get a usable art piece to fit in there.'

Willard Musarurwa

Above: Feeling African, TaTu collection designed in collaboration with Stephen Burks for Artecnica in 2006.

Left: Feeling African, Sallie chair, developed in collaboration with Heidi Lise.

Galerie Arte

Senegal

Joëlle le Bussy was unimpressed by the quality of locally produced furniture and equally horrified at how Africa's precious woods were routinely being exported to Europe to be made into furniture that would then be imported back to Africa to be sold by local retailers. A gallery owner and furniture designer, Le Bussy set out to challenge this practice and prove that high quality furniture and home accessories could be produced locally.

Born in Mont-de-Marsan, France, Le Bussy has lived in Senegal since 1981. She opened her West African art-focused gallery-cum-showroom, Galerie Arte, in Dakar in 1996 and her second, Patio Saint-Louis, in the Northern Senegalese town of Saint-Louis in 2009. Le Bussy's interest in Africa's classical art greatly influences her award-winning furniture designs, which fuse the African and European styles of her multicultural Belgian, Congolese and Senegalese/French heritage. Telling West Africa's creative history through her designs, elements such as masks are inserted into panels, while doors carved by the Dogon, Asante, Baule and Bamun peoples replace conventional ones. Other designs are more contemporary.

Galerie Arte's furniture collections are hand-crafted in the gallery's on-site workshop and Le Bussy is keen to retain the artisanal, handmade aspects of furniture production. She has adapted and combined classic French furniture-assembly techniques with local Senegalese craftsmanship, employing the exceptional skills of carpenters who come from Casamance. Le Bussy primarily works with high-quality West and Central African woods sourced from certified plantations across the continent. Rare woods such as ebony and ronier palm are salvaged from recycled driftwood or discarded woods. Le Bussy also commissions local blacksmiths to create cast iron and bronze handles and fittings, using the lost wax method.

Le Bussy exhibits and sells her designs internationally, and local demand for her designs has increased. Le Bussy has become a design professor at the University Gaston Berger in Saint-Louis. She is also the founder of *Le Fleuve en Couleurs* (*The River of Colours*), a contemporary art festival in Saint-Louis.

'I want to create something that is 100 per cent Senegalese and that is also seen as a luxury product.'

Joëlle le Bussy (ft.com, 2013)

'For me, the charm of African design is that it is not yet industrialized but handmade... I consider the weakness of not being industrialized as a strength as far as design is concerned.'

Joëlle le Bussy

Haldane Martin

South Africa

Haldane Martin is an innovative furniture, product and industrial designer whose classic modern designs serve to connect us harmoniously to the world in which we live. Martin believes that the environments we live in and the objects we choose to surround ourselves with should reflect the core of who we are and how we think about these objects, from our day-to-day interactions, the need for balance and our impact on the environment to simply taking pleasure in them. Martin set up his eponymous studio in 1994; he is based in Cape Town, South Africa.

'A very important part of my work has been about creating furniture objects that embody and contribute towards the development of a new inclusive South African cultural identity.'

Haldane Martin

Martin grew up surrounded by creativity, as his father was in the music industry and his mother in craft. He studied industrial design at Cape Technikon, where 'I was fortunate to have been taught by a number of prominent South African fine artists, which I think has given my design work a bit more depth than if I had been taught by industrial designers.'

Inspired by South Africa's diverse cultural and creative influences, both past and present, Martin's designs also express an emerging South African identity. This is highlighted in products such as his award-winning Zulu Mama chair, inspired by Zulu basket-weaving techniques and making use of recycled plastic woven onto recycled stainless steel frames. Other sources of inspiration include animism and nature, as seen in the Songololo couch. And as a nod to his Scandinavian heritage (his mother is Norwegian), Martin is also drawn to mid-century design heroes such as Alvar Aalto, whose Modernist organic designs inspire the undulating lines of the Baba Papa lounger. Interested in local crafts and traditional production methods, materials and quality are also important to Martin in creating objects that have longevity and reflect human-centred values.

Martin's award-winning designs can be found within the stylish interiors of high-end residential and hospitality properties across the world, and in 2011 a move into interior design saw the company's first large-scale commercial project: Truth Coffee's steampunk-inspired HQ, named 'the world's best coffee shop' by MSN Travel in 2013.

'I believe in creating iconic designs that inspire my fellow human beings and contribute to the evolution of culture.'

Haldane Martin

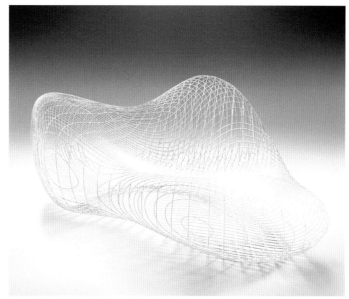

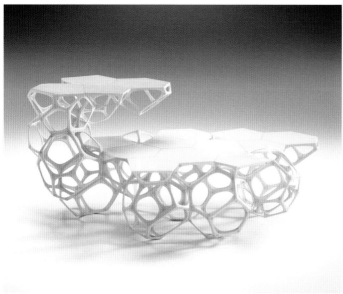

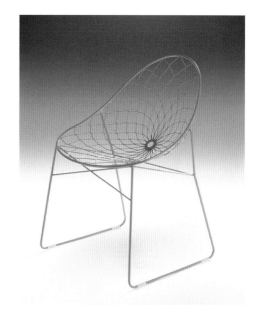

Opposite: Haldane Martin, Zulu Mama cafe chair; the basket expresses the archetypal feminine activity of gathering.

Top left: Haldane Martin, Riempie chair, inspired by early Cape Dutch furniture; solid Kiaat timber with a Malaysian hand-caning weaving pattern.

Top right: Haldane Martin, Baba Papa lounger; inspired by smooth, water-worn pebbles.

Above left: Haldane Martin, Polyhedra coffee table; it is porous and is inspired by the world of organic bone structures revealed by scanning-electron microscope images.

Above right: Haldane Martin, Source wire chair; inspired by phyllotaxis – the spiral growth pattern found in leaf and flower petal arrangements.

Hamed Design

Burkina Faso

'My work is a constant
search to find the right
balance between the
modern and the way
of life in Africa, to find
my own signature.'

Hamed Ouattara

Burkina Faso's contemporary art and design market is relatively young.
Hamed Ouattara, a local fine artist and furniture designer, recognized
the need to help nurture this market for those who are becoming
successful in the industry, whether creators or buyers. In 2000, he
established his studio, Hamed Design, with the intention of promoting
visual art from Burkina Faso to an international audience.

Ouattara sought to help people gain a sense of pride in what was being
designed and manufactured locally, using his designs to counteract the
influx of cheap imports that end up causing the erosion of the country's
artisanal heritage. 'My goal is to provide a key point in a continent which
suffers from imports and all kinds of imitation furniture,' he says, 'especially
that of poor quality, which does not reflect our culture.' This mission
underpins Ouattara's work and he has developed his own technological
production processes based on local artisanal principles.

Ouattara is recognized for his work both as a painter and also as a designer;
each discipline has an impact on the other. Initially self-taught, his creative
interests began as child growing up in Ouagadougou, and in 2003 he went
on to study design at the prestigious design school ENSCI-Les Ateliers in
Paris, returning home after graduation to continue his work. Ouattara sees
himself at the crossroads of two cultures: Africa, welcoming, hot, colourful,
with connections to the earth and each other; and Europe, colder, sanitized,
and centring around the individual. Citing '...life in Africa, the strong
need for development and diversity, and affirmation of my culture' as his
main sources of inspiration, Ouattara's work exhibits a distinctive, bold
aesthetic full of character and colour; his ingenuity lies in his fashioning
of contemporary functional furniture from a range of raw materials that
include discarded metal, plastic and other finished products of the modern

Left: Hamed Design, cabinet,
Design Network Africa, 2013.

Above: Hamed Design, chair,
Design Network Africa, 2013.

Opposite: Hamed Design, cabinet,
Design Network Africa, 2013.

'Design for us [Africa] is a door to the alternative, new creations that can improve our lives while enriching us culturally.'

Hamed Ouattara

world and society's high consumption. These materials give his designs a raw, lived-in look – the worn patina that characterizes his work draws attention to the materials' former life and ultimately tells a story.

Ouattara's belief that design contributes to the wider development of his country has seen him use his studio as a place to bring together local artists from the fields of design, sculpture, painting and installation, providing them with a platform for promotion. Ouattara's workshop also serves as a training facility, where he uses his and his team's skills and experience to provide training for 'young craftsmen and all those who would like to be a designer in my country or elsewhere in Africa.' Ultimately, Ouattara has a greater goal of contributing to the development of the creative sector in his country by creating Burkina Faso's first school of contemporary art.

Hamed Design caters to an African and European clientele, has exhibited widely and is a member of Design Network Africa.

Jean Servais Somian
Côte d'Ivoire · France

'I never thought that I would really be able to make a career out of my passion: I did not know where to start... Nevertheless, the most important thing for me was to create and have those creations exhibited.'

Jean Servais Somian

Jean Servais Somian, a furniture and product designer, and sculptor, started creating furniture in 1999. Somian launched his first furniture and decorative objects collection, 'Azuretti', in honour of the small village in the town of Grand-Bassam, Côte d'Ivoire, where he set up his workshops.

Born and raised in Adiaké, Côte d'Ivoire, Somian trained in carpentry and cabinetmaking at the Georges Ghandour Centre in Abidjan and then in sculpture at the Artisanal Centre in Grand-Bassam. He was later awarded a furniture design internship, which took him to Lausanne, Switzerland. Somian subsequently moved to France and began exploring the world of furniture and product design more seriously, benefitting from the increased exposure his designs were receiving through galleries and exhibitions. He eventually made the decision to follow a career in furniture design during a trip back to Côte d'Ivoire in 1997, and currently divides his time between Paris and Grand-Bassam, where he works with a team of master artisans and cabinet-makers.

Somian's work pays homage to the past, drawing inspiration from West Africa's deep-rooted woodcarving traditions, combining these elements with Western influences. 'This cultural fusion allows me to imagine,' he says, 'to draw and to work the nobility of materials.' Specializing in the art of cabinet-making, wood is Somian's favoured material. He mainly works with coconut wood and is fascinated by the structure of the fibres hidden within the trunk. Other local species he uses include iroko, bete (an African black walnut) and mahogany. Somian works with tools specially created for him by local blacksmiths to hollow out the giant tree trunks, a process that he acknowledges to be time-consuming, but, because it is his passion, it is something he enjoys. Leather, rope, stone and traditional art are some of the other materials and elements he uses to embellish his designs.

Somian has participated in solo and group exhibitions across Africa, and internationally, his work attracting the attention of collectors, institutions, foundations and art galleries. He has also undertaken interior design commissions.

'My furniture, my objects come from the inspiration
of African tradition and Western influence.
The achievement of this cultural fusion allows
me to imagine, to work the materials' nobility.'

Jean Servais Somian

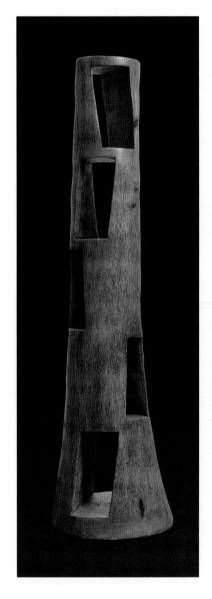

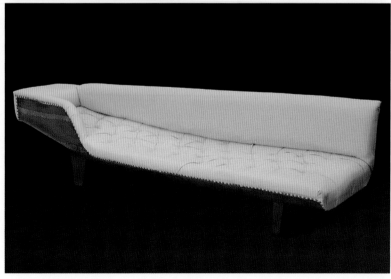

Opposite far left: Jean Servais
Somian, Arbre, bookcase.

Opposite above right: Jean Servais
Somian, coffee table with mirror inset.

Opposite below right: Jean Servais
Somian, Pirogue, couch in yellow.

Below: Jean Servais Somian, Stephy
and Dom, storage unit, closed
and open.

Jomo Design Furniture

Ethiopia · USA

Furniture designer Jomo Tariku looks to the past to create products for the future, drawing inspiration from Africa's woodcarving traditions, centuries-old architecture, his Ethiopian heritage and the influences of a childhood surrounded by creativity.

'For future designers, our rich heritage should be an easy place to find inspiration and would even help an architect or product designer to stand out from the crowd. We need to spend a bit more time learning from our history and reinterpreting what we have learned with our own style.'

Jomo Tariku

Based in Virginia, USA, Tariku was born in Kenya to Ethiopian parents and spent most of his formative years in Ethiopia, where he recalls not having 'to go far for inspiration, growing up, our living room was decorated like a small gallery': filled with the fine furniture and souvenirs his father would bring home from his travels. Tariku has always had an affinity with drawing. Initially interested in pursuing fine arts, he found his calling studying industrial design at the University of Kansas. While researching contemporary African furniture for his final thesis, Tariku noted the absence of contemporary African design in the market and so began to sketch ideas for his own collection.

In 2000, with childhood friend and business partner, Henock Kebede, Tariku launched Jomo Design Furniture (JDF). In 2004, the pair successfully launched JDF's flagship collection, 'Berchuma', which means 'stool or small chair', at the Architectural Digest Home Design Show in New York. It was picked by the Fine Living Network to be profiled on the 'Sheila Bridges: Designer Living' show. 'Berchuma' was designed in collaboration with sculptor and artist Adiskidan Ambaye.

JDF's designs are made from the finest hardwoods, such as maple and walnut, and are characterized by solid, sturdy shapes that retain the feel of classical African furniture: in particular, paying homage to the continent's iconic stools. Observing which elements have evolved, and which ones have stayed the same over time, he seeks to create 'the strong, artistic and mischievous great-great grandchildren of those designs.' Marrying reliability, comfort and practicality with beauty, the designs are adapted to the demands of contemporary living; several designs are multi-functional, serving as seating, end tables or storage. True to his industrial design roots, Tariku makes use of 3D modelling and wood-shop prototyping.

'We have not lost sight of the fact that the fundamentals of good furniture design have been with us for centuries.'

Jomo Tariku

Left: Jomo Furniture Design, The Axum Chair, inspired by architectural styles of the city of Axum in Ethiopia.

Below left: Jomo Furniture Design, Ensera stool, named after the Ethiopian word for a pot-bellied water jug.

Below centre: Jomo Furniture Design, The Stack, based on the clean and graceful lines of traditional three-legged African stools.

Below right: Jomo Furniture Design, The Ruby, inspired by the precious jewel.

Khmissa

Morocco · Germany

'We want to elevate our products beyond the scope of classical arts and crafts.'

Bettina Lamghari el Kossori

Old discarded tyres usually end up in landfills where they can remain for decades if not centuries because they are not biodegradable. Taking this universal product, which in Morocco is burnt in ceramic ovens releasing harmful toxins into the air, Khmissa salvages the rubber and turns it into functional furniture and home accessories that display the skill and ingenuity of Moroccan artisans.

Khmissa is a small family business that was started in 2002 by Bettina and Said Lamghari el Kossori and is operated between Marrakech, Said's home country, and Munich where the couple live. Bettina is a professional studio photographer, who specializes in food and lifestyle photography, and Said was a merchant in the souks of Marrakech, and they have dedicated their expertise to developing Moroccan handicrafts to the level of quality required in the global market. All Khmissa's products are produced in Morocco, made by hand in collaboration with local artisans and artists; Bettina notes that, 'in Morocco there is a great dynamic between designers and handworkers.'

Khmissa's designs are inspired by the traditions of Moroccan lifestyle and contemporary design aesthetics, combining classical techniques with unexpected materials such as tyres. The reclaimed rubber is applied to forms made from recycled wood, the grooves of the tread forming the decorative patterns. The artisans etch intricate patterns based on local traditions. The Lamghari el Kossoris also experiment with the application of gold and silver leaf finishes to the finished furniture, which enhances the patterns and brings a touch of glamour. In addition, Khmissa produce classically inspired Moroccan glassware and colourful Berber rugs made by Berber women using recycled strips of fabric as a substitute for weaving with wool, which is costly.

Khmissa's products are carried by high-end stores around the globe and the company also works with interior designers to create unique commissioned designs.

Opposite: Khmissa,
rubber tables.

Below: Khmissa,
rubber storage chest.

Right: Khmissa, rubber stools,
in gold and silver finishes.

'We take a poor material, which
is locally burnt in ceramic ovens
releasing harmful toxins into the air,
and turn it into functional products.'

Bettina Lamghari el Kossori

Nulangee Design
Senegal

'Everything is
connected to nature.'

Babacar Mbodj Niang

A love of creating objects since childhood led Senegalese artist, sculptor and designer Babacar Mbodj Niang to pursue a career in the arts, despite family objections.

Self-taught, Niang launched Nulangee Design in 1986, setting up his studio in Rufisque, a Senegalese town 15 miles from Dakar, the country's bustling capital city.

Niang is drawn to nature, a defining characteristic of his elegant, organic designs and the choice of found and natural materials he works with to produce them. He experiments with combining different materials, including wood, iron and ox horn, adding textures and visual interest through the inclusion of additional elements such as woven, braided and moulded leather. Mostly working alone, from time to time Niang collaborates with other artisans, sharing the skills required for specific projects.

In tune with the materials he uses, Niang seeks to do more than simply create an item of furniture and works to reveal the true value of the wood: its personality. Niang's designs, in particular his carved wood furniture, are infused with a lifelike quality that often gives the viewer glimpses of the characters within them. Niang's designs fuel the imagination, conjuring up images of, for instance, animals crossing the savannah, the gangly legs of a giraffe, a feline predator poised to pounce, or hints of an elderly wise man reclining in his chair, inviting you to sit with him awhile.

Niang's designs have been showcased internationally and have drawn the attention of collectors from around the world. Nulangee Design is a member of Design Network Africa.

Above left: Nulangee Design,
chair, Design Network Africa,
2013.

Above right: Nulangee
Design, Vertebres chair in
ebony, Design Network Africa,
2013.

Opposite: Nulangee Design,
ebony and wood benches,
Design Network Africa, 2013.

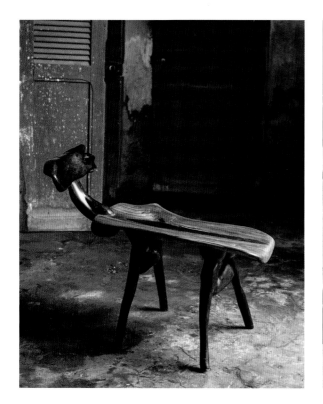

Ousmane Mbaye Design

Senegal

Thirty proved to be a turning-point for Senegalese furniture designer Ousmane Mbaye, experiencing what he calls his 'thirties crisis'. After spending 15 years managing and working in his father's refrigeration repair workshop, Mbaye felt it was time for a change.

Mbaye grew up in the Medina district of Senegal's capital city, Dakar. The area is home to many artisans and workshops, but aside from drawing and tinkering about with found objects, Mbaye had never really considered a career in design himself. However, as doubts about continuing as a refrigeration mechanic began to set in, he started to take his growing interest in art and design more seriously. In 2005, Mbaye followed his dream and set up a workshop in Soumbedioune, Dakar, where along with a team of 15 full-time workers, he creates furniture pieces that he affectionately refers to as his 'paintings'.

Referring to himself as the 'King of Recycling', Mbaye finds the beauty in reusable discarded materials such as oil barrel lids, sheets of metal and galvanized iron pipes, reworking them into functional, distinctive works of art. Mbaye's work is a reflection of Africa's resourcefulness and ingenuity in the way that discarded materials have long been collected and turned into products with renewed purpose. Mbaye's choice of materials came out of necessity, using whatever he could find; many of the materials he uses come from foreign imports and are associated with pollution as they end up blighting the landscape.

Mbaye's years of working with freezers and refrigerators, cable reels and switches has given him the necessary technical expertise to bring his ideas to life, also lending his products an industrial edge. The linear abstract forms of his designs are accentuated with bright flashes of colour courtesy of the original finishes on the metals used, bringing a touch of warmth to the cold, hard edges. Colours and materials are harmoniously combined to create objects that are both beautiful and useful.

Mbaye seeks to design products that cannot be confined by boundaries, saying that while 'African design' is rooted in Africa, it is also universal and

'For me, metal was a means to expand my horizons; to think differently.'

Ousmane Mbaye
(African Lookbook)

'I had my "thirties crisis"
and I decided to do something
that really appealed to me,
something different.'

Ousmane Mbaye

Opposite: Ousmane Mbaye
Design, Tonton chair.

Above: Ousmane Mbaye
Design, Patrimoine stools
and table.

Right: Ousmane Mbaye
Design, Mosaic, two-door
sideboard.

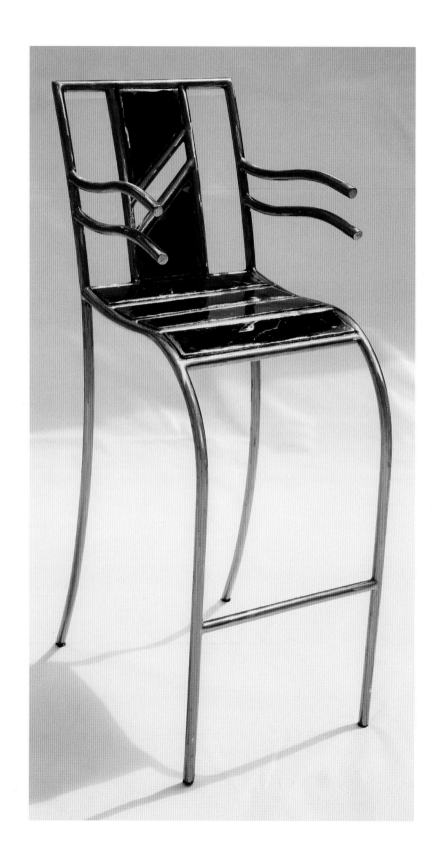

Right: Ousmane Mbaye Design,
Patrimoine, bar stool.

Opposite: Ousmane Mbaye Design,
five-door sideboard.

'At first, I worked with whatever materials were within my reach – drums of petrol, old water pipes that I found around town. It was easier for me this way because I didn't have a lot of money at the time to buy material. In hindsight, I've come to realize that all materials are noble. It all depends on what you do with them and on the importance that you give them.'

Ousmane Mbaye (African Lookbook)

contemporary, so in effect, 'There is no such thing as "African Design", but there are "African Designers".'

Mbaye's designs have been exhibited internationally and were included in the landmark exhibition *The Global Africa Project*. Mbaye's furniture practice extends to interior design, bringing his recycling aesthetic to hospitality interiors around the country.

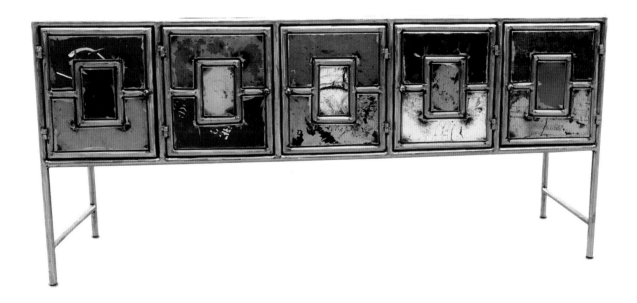

Tekura

Ghana

Tekura is an award-winning producer of hand-crafted furniture and decor that is imbued with the spirit of Ghana's rich artistic culture and heritage. Based in the capital, Accra, the company was founded in 2000 by Josephine Forson and her husband, Kweku.

'[Our work] is an attempt to posture and preserve traditional Ghanaian art and craft in contemporary form.'

Josephine Forson

Self-taught in the art of furniture design and production, Josephine Forson's venture into the field began during a five-year stint working for an Aid to Artisans Ghana programme. It sparked a strong interest in exploring ways of turning some of the country's classical arts and crafts into modern, functional pieces, while helping to preserve Ghana's classical craft heritage.

Drawing inspiration from Ghana's ancient majestic cultures such as the Asante and Fanti, Tekura's designs are stylish interpretations of iconic classical symbols such as the celebrated Asante stool. Tekura has also collaborated with Malian designer Cheick Diallo on a range called 'Design Line'. Developed specifically for the high-end market, the range features the aptly titled 'Walking Tables', which stand tall and elegant, and yet exude a touch of playfulness.

The Forsons have developed their own unique furniture production techniques, working in partnership with highly skilled local artisans contracted to the production workshop. The artisans are offered training, technical assistance and a safe working environment. Upholding a respect for the environment in which they live and work, Tekura's wooden pieces are crafted from selected pieces of wood, mainly cedrela (*cedar*), which is found lying on the ground following reforestation. Other recycled materials such as metal are also used.

Their commitment to ensuring that every piece produced is of exceptional quality has earned Tekura an international following. The company's designs are carried by selected high-end stores across Europe and North America, in addition to their Accra-based shop and gallery. Tekura's work has been exhibited widely, at *Ambiente*, Germany and *Graphic Africa*, UK, for instance, as a member of Design Network Africa.

'We focus on providing our clients all over the world with our beautifully crafted furniture pieces and decorative accessories portraying the heritage and culture of the African people.'

Kweku and Josephine Forson

Yinka Ilori

Nigeria · UK

> 'My work is not just furniture, but art that you can appreciate over time.'
>
> *Yinka Ilori*

Dismantling discarded and unwanted pieces of furniture and reassembling the pieces to create entirely new silhouettes characterizes the work of Yinka Ilori, a London-based furniture designer. Ilori, who founded his eponymous design studio in 2012, specializes in sustainable design by upcycling.

Colourful and often quirky, each one of Ilori's creations is based on taking a traditional Nigerian parable and conveying its sentiments through brightly painted wood, paired with vibrant patterns and fabrics that bring to life the once unloved furniture pieces. Using traditional Nigerian parables and the fabrics that he grew up with as a child, Ilori connects with his Nigerian heritage. 'My parents shared Nigerian parables with me daily,' he says. 'I never understood the importance and symbolism of these parables, but as time went on and I grew older I started to understand why my parents shared these with me. It was because they loved me and wanted to share something special with me.'

Ilori's interest in upcycling unwanted furniture began while at London Metropolitan University studying for a BA in product design and furniture. Ilori worked on a group project titled 'Our Chair', where each group had to dismantle the chairs provided and then redesign the pieces into new furniture that had a different meaning and function. Ilori said, 'That was when I fell in love with upcycling and wanted to become an upcycle designer who told meaningful, yet humorous stories.' Fuelled by this interest in finding creative solutions to challenge the unnecessary waste in modern consumer societies, Ilori works towards helping to effect positive change. He happily accepts unwanted or damaged furniture from private individuals, upcycling any piece of furniture through which he can tell a story.

Ilori has exhibited his creations widely, including in Milan, Germany, New York, Nigeria and Sweden. He also runs workshops from his studio and at design events, where he gives members of the public the chance to upcycle their own chair.

Each caption represents the Nigerian parable that inspires the corresponding chair's design; the captions are written in Yoruba with accompanying translations.

1. OSUMARE
Bí a ti ńṣe ní'bi kan èèwọ ` ibòmíràn ni.
(What is acceptable in one place is an abomination in another.)

'From an early age we [Yinka and his siblings] were exposed to such a beautiful culture that has inspired the designer that I am today.'

Yinka Ilori

2. THE ABIKE COLLECTION
Iya Onígbá ló ńfi igbá ẹ̀ kó ilẹ̀ tí wọ́
n fi ńpèé ní àkárágbá. (The owner that packs
rubbish with his calabash made others treat
it as broken.)

3. EWA
Àtùpà kì í níyì lọ́ọ̀ sán.
(A lamp is not valued in the afternoons.
There's always a right time.)

4. KEKERE
Bí ojú ò bá fọ́ ẹsẹ̀ kìí ṣìnà.
(If the eyes are not blind, the legs won't
miss the way. Vision is critical: you can't
get what you can't see.)

5. OBA
Ẹni tí yóò dáṣọ ẹtù inú rẹ̀ níí gbé.
(Whoever plans to acquire an expensive
cloth will keep it to himself. Keep your
lofty dreams to yourself.)

6. IJOKO AGBA
Tí ẹ̀ dá bá mọ iṣẹ́ àṣelà ni, iwọ ̀nba ni làálàá
máa mọ. (If a man knows for sure what his
destined path to success is, he will hustle less.)

7. OBA KEKERE
Àgbá òfìfo ló ńpariwo, èyí tó lómi nínú kì í dún.
(It's empty vessels that are noisy; those filled
with water are not.)

4.

5.

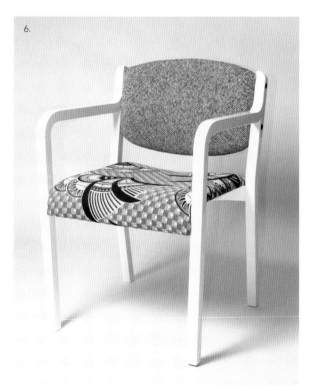

6.

7.

Lighting & Decor

Beautifying living and working spaces, the interior accessories showcased here thoughtfully address the demands and impacts of modern living and lifestyles across the continent, and beyond, in ways that are decorative, sustainable and functional.

Playing with textures, old and new techniques are combined in ways that elevate the crafts of the roadside artisan and modernize ancient traditions. Wood is skilfully turned into sleek sculptural pieces, while seeds and beads are painstakingly woven into commanding, functional wall features. Precious metals draw attention to majestic kingdoms of the past and enhance the sense of luxury that comes with exquisite craftsmanship and attention to detail. Lighting sees natural materials such as clay transformed into soulful, earthy products, reflections of the earth from which they are formed, while highly sophisticated mesmerizing light installations and atmospheric lamp collections bring a touch of theatre to the interior space.

Drawing attention to the need for people to recycle more, once again found and discarded materials are creatively re-imagined into stylish functional objects, such as the recycling of plastic bottles and glass wine bottles into playful lighting and stylish containers.

Centro de Arte Africana

Mozambique

Centro de Arte Africana is a family business that was founded by Carlos Mondlane in 1992, with the aim of developing and promoting Mozambique's woodcarving heritage. Mondlane is himself an accomplished craftsman; he started out in the industry in 1980 and later began selling the handicrafts of his fellow woodcarvers.

'[Our aim is to] show the country and the world that it is possible to create sustainable and private companies in the business of craft.'

Carlos Mondlane

Serving as both a production centre and export facility, Centro de Arte Africana was set up by Mondlane with the help of a local Aid to Artisans programme with which he was working at the time. It was in response to increasing demand for local woodcarvings and the realization that his own production output could not meet demand. Today, Centro de Arte Africana represents highly skilled and experienced carvers throughout the country, including Nampula Province and the Miombo Woodlands. The woodcarvers Mondlane works with produce a range of over 300 finely hand-crafted wood products, including functional decorative objects, jewelry and musical instruments. The teams of craftsmen work with precious raw woods, including sustainably sourced sandalwood, rosewood, jambirre, cimbirre and mpingo, a dark hardwood also known as African blackwood, Mozambican ebony and zebrawood, depending on the region. Mpingo grows along Mozambique's coastal forests and in the Miombo Woodlands. This dark wood enhances the elegant, striking silhouettes of the product designs, giving them a metal-like finish.

Mondlane is committed to encouraging innovation in production techniques and product design, and his efforts have won the company several awards. Centro de Arte Africana has also exhibited widely and is currently the largest exporter of Mozambican handicrafts internationally. Mondlane's extensive experience in the sector led to his appointment as Chairman of Mozambique's National Association of Craftsmen.

'[Our] production is
guaranteed by a highly
qualified and experienced
team of craftsmen working
with precious raw material.'

Carlos Mondlane

Heath Nash

South Africa

Heath Nash is an environmentally conscious designer who turns post-consumer waste into innovative, captivating products, with a distinctly playful edge. The designer, who set up his studio in 2004, graduated from the University of Cape Town with a BA in fine art, majoring in sculpture.

'People are generally quite shocked that those things are made from rubbish, which I find really pleasing. That shows that I'm obviously doing it right and that's exactly the point I am trying to make! It is possible to re-use this kind of plastic straight away and take it to a sophisticated level.'

Heath Nash

In his final year at university Nash began to develop his signature techniques, utilizing what he defines as 'a very playful and experimental way of dealing with simple materials, and basically found the work process that I still employ today – the process of trial and error.' Immersed in this process, Nash began to play with one of South Africa's, and indeed the continent's, widely utilized local craft materials: galvanized steel wire. During this period he met a local wire artist, Richard Mandongwe, who was selling flowers made from old plastic bottles and wire. Nash began working with Mandongwe, integrating his wire skills with what he dubbed 'an amazing new material', bottle plastic, in his own experimental process. This signalled a new direction for Nash and gave rise to a collection of repurposed post-consumer plastic waste products, which Nash entitled 'Other People's Rubbish' .

For Nash, working with discarded waste was a way of promoting sustainable solutions and instilling the idea of recycling in what he felt was a very unaware South African public: using the wire and plastic to communicate his message, while devising a new aesthetic combining contemporary design with local skills. It was an aesthetic that 'spoke to the then current South African situation, given a growing discussion at the time around forging a new national identity through design.'

Nash's designs have won him prestigious awards including *Elle Decoration* South Africa, Designer and Lighting Designer of the Year, 2006, the British

Council's Creative Entrepreneur of the Year (SA),
2006, and an eco-lighting award judged by Ingo
Maurer at Finland's premier interiors show, *Habitare*,
in 2010. In a bid to promote productive learning
exchange opportunities, Nash has also collaborated
with several designers and craft organizations in and
around Southern Africa. This has seen him work
with the Binga Craft Centre in Zimbabwe and fellow
Design Network Africa members Marjorie Wallace
of Mutapo and Kitengela Glass from Kenya.

'I love to make things.
I always have.'

Heath Nash

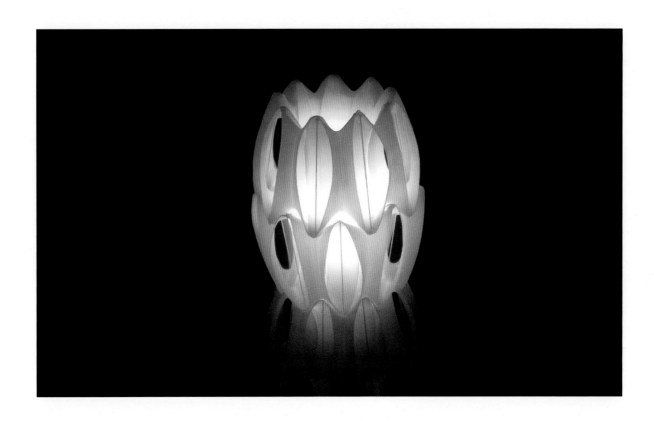

Opposite: Master Wire and
Bead Craft, sunburst clock
and beaded mirror.

Master Wire
and Bead Craft
Zimbabwe · South Africa

**Bishop Tarambawamwe grew up in Rusape, Zimbabwe, where,
in between herding cattle and attending school, he and his friends
would play around with beads and wire, creating cars and other toys,
never once imagining that this pastime would lead to a successful
future career as a wire artist.**

*'I never thought of
my wirework as art.
I just wanted to earn
an income, until one
day a man commented
that our products were
masterpieces. That
changed my own view
of my work.'*

*Bishop Tarambawamwe
(CCDI)*

After completing his schooling, Tarambawamwe moved to South Africa
in 2002, first settling in Pretoria and then moving to Cape Town in 2004.
There he began to create and sell wire sculptures in a bid to make a living,
adapting his designs to reflect the tastes of his new home. Tarambawamwe
soon teamed up with a fellow wire artist, Tawanda Dengedza, and together
the pair began making and selling their creations at traffic lights along
Cape Town's main roads. Tarambawamwe's products proved popular with
tourists and locals alike, something that did not go unnoticed, and soon
he was offered a stall at the V&A Waterfront's Craft Market, Cape Town's
upmarket shopping and leisure destination. From there, Tarambawamwe
formally launched his company, Master Wire and Bead Craft, in 2005 and
soon after joined the Cape Craft and Design Institute (CCDI). Membership
brought with it exposure to other crafters, along with mentoring and
business and product development opportunities that enabled his business
to grow exponentially. With the help of the CCDI, Tarambawamwe has
made the transition into sophisticated interior decor accessories.

Tarambawamwe's designs are inspired by his culture and traditions:
the grazing cows from his early childhood, nature, and his surroundings.
These inspirations are evident in his designs, for instance in the striking
black-and-white beaded mirror which reaches almost a metre in diameter,
in whose beaded pattern the distinctive stippled markings of the
Nguni cow hide are skilfully replicated. Wirework and beading is labour
intensive, so, depending on size, it can take between one and two days
to complete the design. Tarambawamwe and his team use glass beads
and an indigenous seed, traditionally used by people in the rural areas
to aid teething. Exhibited and sold both locally and internationally,
Tarambawamwe's designs have attracted commissions from the high-
end retail and hospitality sectors, and can be found in private homes.

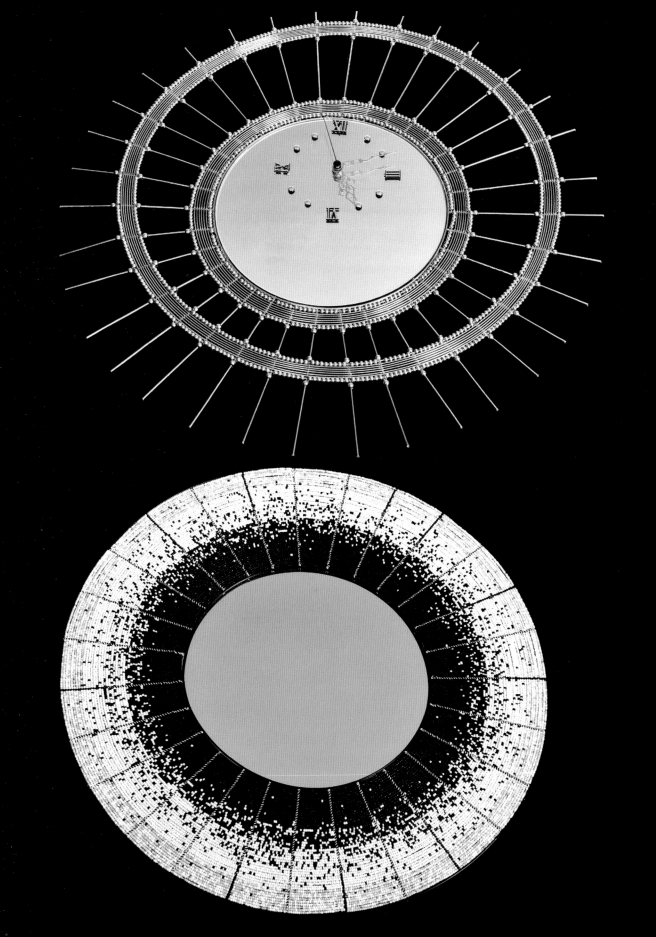

Michou Bowls

South Africa

South African artist Michou started out in 1984 as the co-founder of a bespoke furniture company based in Cape Town, and it was while looking for a unique handmade gift to give to a valued client that she struck upon the idea of water-gilding the hand-carved wooden bowls typically sold by the roadside to tourists.

Water-gilding is an ancient North African technique: a highly skilled, labour-intensive process of transferring thin leaves of gold onto wooden objects. The technique was invented more than 5,500 years ago by the ancient Egyptians and has passed on to many cultures through the ages.

Largely self-taught, it has taken Michou more than 15 years to develop the skills, having gradually learnt the rudiments of the craft 'by quasi remote control', courtesy of one of her best friends, Andrea 'Pudi' Crasemann. Lessons took place during yearly holidays when Pudi, who lives in Hamburg, came to visit family in Cape Town and Michou went to visit family in Hamburg. Michou initially began practising on items that had historically been gilded, for instance lamp bases and mirror frames. She successfully applied the technique to wooden bowls and soon began to work with local artisans, who carved the bowls she required using local woods including jacaranda, wild olive, and Zimbabwean and Indonesian teak. Echoing her learning process, Michou's product development follows an organic process: as she says, 'Everything we make is our distillation of history, trial and error and luck.' This approach has resulted in an ever-evolving range of unique, serial-numbered bowls marketed under the name Michou Bowls.

Michou works with gold and silver. It is melted, milled, beaten and hand-lifted into booklets of ultra-thin leaves, so that it is ready for application onto the wooden surfaces. Bringing a touch of colour to the bowls, casein paint is also applied: it is either left matt or burnished to a high polish.

'My bowls have no function other than to please the eye. In their imperfection lies their beauty.'

Michou

'I work with different artisans
and am very driven to share skills.
Almost every human being has
something to teach another.'

Michou

The finish of the wood is just as important as the water-gilding or paint application. The bowls are either oiled or waxed to a high shine or left as raw as the original carver made them.

Since gold and silver are precious metals and the water-gilding process is so precise and complex, water-gilding has historically been applied to precious objects. It has usually been reserved for formal or grand places such as churches and palaces or for frames for valuable paintings.

By consciously choosing to adorn the very simply carved, raw wooden objects Michou has broken away from this concept, 'The wooden bowls in themselves are precious. They are part of African history.' And as such they bring together revered traditions of North and Southern Africa.

'The gilded bowls bring
Northern Africa and Southern
Africa together in the
juxtaposition of constructed
formality against relatively
spontaneous carving work.'

Michou

Mud Studio

South Africa

Literally born out of the earth, the majestic chandeliers from Mud Studio exude rustic charm. They are made up of over 6,000 handmade clay beads, which are formed from the surrounding South African soil and hand-crafted in partnership with artisans from the local communities.

'We don't really use any special techniques except special hands, as every single item is handmade.'

Werner du Toit

Inspired by the landscape and nature, the ceramic beads are made from recycled clay and are wire-wrapped, strung and styled around handmade wire frames. The intensive collaborative process lasts over a week and a half, and the materials are passed through the hands of approximately 25 people.

Situated in South Africa's Eastern Free State, Mud Studio was started in 1999 by Philippa du Toit. She and her husband, Werner, went on to build a successful ceramics studio. Werner is Mud Studio's head designer and is responsible for developing products such as the company's signature chandeliers. Werner studied graphic design at a local art school and after spending five years working in the industry, first in Johannesburg and then in London, returned to South Africa to follow his passion of working with clay. It was at a clay supplier shortly after his return that he met Philippa.

The driving force behind Werner's designs is the need for beauty in the things that surround us and when creating Mud Studio's collections he is inspired by 'practical things, yet designs that evoke emotion.' The designs produced include dinnerware, furniture and decor, utilizing production processes that adapt to suit the projects at hand, with in-house teams ranging from two to 40 people depending on the need. Mud Studio also works with other designers whose styles complement the studio's distinctive aesthetic.

Mud Studio's elegant and earthy designs are sold all over the world. And in the face of growing international demand, the couple have resisted pressures to employ mass-production techniques, instead preferring to continue working with their local communities.

People of the Sun

Malawi

People of the Sun (PS) is a social enterprise based in Malawi that works to connect local artisans with business and product development and the marketplace. PS produces a range of hand-crafted homeware collections with global appeal, while reflecting and highlighting local indigenous skills and traditions.

'Everything I do is filled with passion, honesty and a drive to make the world a better place through design!'

Maria Haralambidou

Embracing the motto of 'caring and style', PS's aim is to enable the preservation of local craft, which is increasingly being replaced by industrial alternatives, while also giving artisans a platform to create long-lasting businesses to generate sustainable incomes. All proceeds from trade are reinvested into the organization's social mission. PS was started in November 2012 by British-trained architect Maria Haralambidou. Haralambidou's interest in social enterprise began in 2011 with her involvement in a community basket-weaving project in Zimbabwe, which enabled her to experience first hand the potential of using design as a means of aiding sustainable development for disadvantaged communities.

Collaboration is at the heart of PS. Haralambidou designs many of the initial ideas, which are then developed hand in hand with the relevant artisans through a series of prototypes on-site. Collaboration also extends to working with carefully selected international designers and architects (see page 12). At a local level, development of the Blantyre Jar, one of the organization's signature products, brought together three local groups. Haralambidou was inspired when she met Jarvis of Zochita Zambiri enterprise. He is a local artisan who uses a rudimentary process of hand-cutting discarded wine bottles, collected from hotels and restaurants, with twine to create drinking glasses for his community. Haralambidou worked with Jarvis to refine the design and create a commercially appealing product for a global market: the glass is fitted with machine-lathed hardwood lids using locally sourced mahogany.

Haralambidou has also been approached to design local buildings, reworking traditional construction techniques, in addition to creating interiors for upscale cafes, restaurants and homes centred around the PS style and philosophy. In 2014, Haralambidou and PS were honoured at the inaugural Africa Design Award ceremony in Gabon.

willowlamp
South Africa

'My creative process is
about understanding
and distilling the essence
of what makes nature
and then crystallizing
and reflecting it back
into reality through
the filter of heightened
pure abstract form.'

Adam Hoets

The formation of willowlamp was an organic process: co-founder Adam Hoets, a South African eco-architect, shared ideas as he experimented with the creation of curtains from ball chains, looking for an effective solution to aid the suspension.

The answer came in the form of the simple yet ingenious idea of creating a tiny notch in laser-cut steel frames to make a fastener-free chain curtain system. For Hoets, the patented system unleashed endless design possibilities and, after months of research and development, 2005 saw the completion of the first willowlamp light.

Every light piece comprises hundreds of chain strands, each meticulously hand-assembled using components that are either cut and shaped by hand or industrially manufactured off-site. Belying the solid framework that holds them all together, from a distance the lighting constructions look as if they have been spun from silken strands. The intricately arranged chains form dazzling patterns that gently shift with changes in the surrounding air, giving willowlamp's chandeliers an ethereal quality. The dynamic, organic forms are multifaceted and change their appearance depending on the viewer's position. When viewed from the side, the shimmering ball chain strands form a gently cascading curtain, while standing underneath and looking up provides a totally different perspective, rather like the patterns seen through a kaleidoscope. In the case of the award-winning 'Flower of Life' chandelier they are not unlike the patterns of woven baskets. Geometry and nature – flowers in particular – are a major source of inspiration for Hoets, with distinctive forms such as frangipani blooms, fuchsia flowers, seashells and the protea, South Africa's national flower, evident in some of designs, along with Islamic patterns and Chinese lanterns.

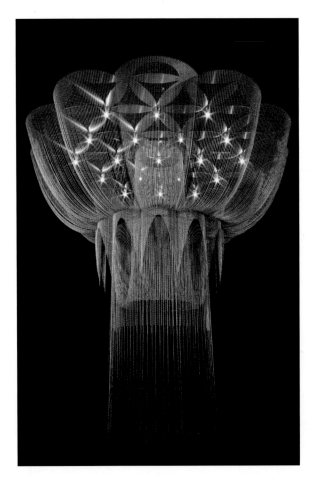

Originally based in Johannesburg, willowlamp
now operates from a studio and workshop at the
foot of the majestic Table Mountain in Cape Town,
and in addition to chandeliers also produces illuminated
sculptural art pieces. From its inception, the company
has won several prestigious awards and has showcased
their products at numerous design fairs and exhibitions,
both locally and internationally.

Above left: willowlamp, Flower
of Life chandelier, willowlamp's
original award-winning design
based on the sacred geometry
of the flower of life.

Above right: willowlamp,
Mandala: white diamond light
sculpture inspired by Islamic
patterns.

Opposite: willowlamp, Fuschia
chandelier, based on the form
of fuschia flowers.

YSWARA

South Africa

'It was my dream to
capture true African
luxury. I always believed
that there is a magic
to Africa... its
craftsmanship and
inspiration are at
the very foundation
of luxury.'

Swaady Martin-Leke

**YSWARA is a premier luxury tea brand that is inspired by Africa's
ancient tea drinking traditions. YSWARA invokes the pride and
sophistication of Africa's traditions and cultures.**

YSWARA, based in Johannesburg, South Africa, was launched in December
2012 by Swaady Martin-Leke, who had observed that although Africa was a
leading exporter of tea, there were no luxury tea brands coming from the
continent. Appointing itself as the 'curator of precious African teas', YSWARA
offers an adventurous journey into the legends and rich histories that have
captivated the continent for centuries, through the creation of sublime teas
and infusions, named after pre-colonial African kingdoms, queens, natural
wonders and values.

The thought, care and attention to detail that have gone into creating an
exceptional tea drinking experience extend to the creation of a complementary
range of luxury accessories. These have been designed by Martin-Leke, working
in partnership with some of Africa's top creative talents and, in doing so,
upholding the company's mission to 'promote and preserve Africa's rich culture
and history through exceptional products made with our natural resources by
African artisans'. YSWARA's product range sees the delicate designs of the 'Wake
Mia' spoon collection, inspired by nature and crafted from organic materials
gilded in gold alloy. Rooibos tea bush twigs are connected to poppy seed pods
and unfurled jacaranda pods designed to measure the perfect quantity of tea.
Tapping into the traditions of the past, including that of Martin-Leke's Ivorian
heritage, the 'Wake Mia' collection recalls the earthly origins of tea and the
traditions of the Dan people of Liberia and Côte d'Ivoire who carved wooden
'Wake Mia' spoons for ceremonial feasts. Resplendent in black porcelain, the
Sankofa teaset references Africa's written traditions in the form of iconic Adinkra
symbols. YSWARA teas and accessories are sold locally and internationally.

Zenza

Egypt · The Netherlands

Zenza is a home and personal accessories boutique started in 1993 by Dutch national Karin Willems, a creative therapy graduate who sought to start a business combining travelling with creativity after a career working with 'beads and textiles' for several design companies.

'We always define our style as urban nomadic, or souk-aholic. Anyway, words can't describe what we try to put into our designs, but people recognize that our handmade products have some sort of "soul".'

Karin Willems

Willems met her Egyptian partner, Hussein Attia, while on a trip to Egypt to source interesting accessories for Zenza. Attia had studied social science, but was always interested in creating and designing. Over 20 years later Willems and Attia, who reside in Cairo, have transformed Zenza into a sought-after brand of beautifully crafted interior and personal products. In 2009, Yasmina Chahbar became Zenza's third partner. Zenza's partners view their role as new generation silk route traders, travelling from country to country, seeking influence from the crafts and traditions they encounter, and bringing the resulting products to trade shows from where they find their way across the globe. As Willems states, this 'is the modern way of the silk route.'

Inspired by the rich heritage of classical Arabic and Indian design, Zenza strives to bring a modern look and feel to classical crafts, and places great value in hand-craftsmanship: a defining characteristic of their designs. In keeping with a desire to make the products refined for modern homes, yet keeping the past in mind, elaborate ancient crafts and artisanal techniques from the past are incorporated into product shapes that adhere to a simple and clean aesthetic. Zenza's main product range comprises lighting, hand-crafted in their Cairo-based factory, as well as furniture and home textiles, both produced in India. Believing that a beautiful product should also have a long life is part of Zenza's sustainable approach to doing business, and as a result the materials used are always selected for durability and pureness. Zenza is especially known for its atmospheric lamp collections which are

Below: Zenza, Princess
Fan table lamp.

Opposite: Zenza, purple
and turquoise coasters.

made from silver-plated or oxidized copper and brass,
and are characterized by the hammering techniques and
intricately detailed punched hole patterns typical of
Egypt's longstanding metalwork traditions.

Zenza's operations and team are divided between Egypt
and the Netherlands. Chahbar runs Zenza's operations in
the Netherlands, where the office, warehouse and shops
are based. Willems describes Zenza as a chain of people
linked together, each with a vital contribution towards
the success of the business. According to her, it is all about
collaboration, 'Sometimes we need the technical support
of craftsmen, because we have the ideas but don't always
have the know-how to create the product.'

'It is vital for us to build
lasting relations with
the craftsmen we work
with. We respect their
knowledge highly and
we are always proud
to be able to keep the
handicraft alive in a world
where mass production
is mainstream.'

Karin Willems

Left: Sabahar textiles handwoven in Ethiopia using natural fibres.

Textiles

Textiles are probably Africa's most expressive artform, given their many highly visible roles in everyday life. Cloths have long been used as records of Africa's histories and traditions, and are still the media through which the stories of an evolving continent are being told, as contemporary textile designers and artisans develop their own African-inspired textiles, or experiment with traditional techniques.

Contemporary textile designs are used to comment on important social issues, or simply to reflect the energy of modern urban life. Designers also seek to combine centuries-old techniques such as block printing with modern methods such as digital printing.

Textiles also see a return to natural production processes as contemporary dye masters seek to preserve such ancient techniques such as natural indigo and *bògòlanfini*. Unlikely materials, including felt, vegetable fibres and bark cloth, are innovatively applied to soft furnishings. And in an industry that was once the domain of men, more women are pioneering the revival and evolution of classical weaving techniques; from Ethiopia to Mauritania they are increasingly threatened by lack of interest and mass production, but they are adapting their skills for contemporary living.

Aboubakar Fofana

Mali

Aboubakar Fofana is a multifaceted artist whose work moves seamlessly between that of the designer and the master artisan. As one of the foremost practitioners of traditional West African indigo and *bògòlanfini* (mud cloth) techniques, Fofana is renowned for his work in natural textiles and is sought after not only to exhibit his work, but also to share his skills, conducting workshops around the world.

'The process of making and working with real indigo is time-consuming and no stage can be skipped or shortened. Understanding how to build a vat and produce consistent and deep colours has taken me many years, and I am still learning.'

Aboubakar Fofana

Born in Mali, Fofana moved to France at a very young age. He developed an interest in design in his early teens and trained as a graphic designer, specializing in calligraphy and hand-lettering. As time went on, Fofana became increasingly interested in the process of natural indigo dyeing.

Introduced to indigo as a young boy, Fofana recalls spending 'time each year in my father's village in Guinea, where I was told about these green leaves that could make a blue colour', but, as he noted, by then natural indigo dyeing had all but disappeared. Fofana has mostly worked in fibre and textile design since the late 1990s, dedicating much of his time to learning the process of natural indigo dyeing – seeking out people who still practised the traditional technique in Mali. Those he found, however, would add chemical indigo powder to their indigo vats rather than using the natural dye process. Undeterred, he turned to literature, where he found descriptions of the process. He had to teach himself and, Fofana notes, 'It was a long and slow apprenticeship where I had to experiment with what information I could find.' Recognition of Fofana's efforts came in 1999 when he was awarded a design scholarship, taking up a residency in Japan with a project named 'Sublime Indigo: Japon, France, Mali', refining his technique in a skills exchange with a dye master.

The traditional techniques Fofana uses take time and are labour intensive, which makes his textiles exclusive as they cannot be mass produced. Even

142

'If you don't have passion it is impossible to continue. Passion is the key to why I do what I do.'

Aboubakar Fofana

when custom-made designs are created, they are only produced in small limited-edition collections. All Fofana's products, from the dyeing process to the finished product, are handmade in Mali, where his studio and workshop are based. Fofana is actively involved in keeping Mali's local textile industries alive. He works with 100% pure organic Malian cotton, which is locally hand-spun and hand-woven by elderly women skilled in spinning the yarn and using the traditional looms. This is a very important element of his production. Fofana would like to see more local processing of the crop, given that a large percentage of Mali's raw cotton is exported. Fofana has also invested in teaching a younger generation the skills, saving them for future generations: 'I am working to preserve this lost memory... this lost tradition of indigo dyeing in West Africa.' To teach and help others Fofana needed to create a sustainable business, so he began creating products from the textiles to sell, helping those he works with to earn a living.

Fofana also collaborates with leading designers, including Aïssa Dione, Donna Karan and Edun, as well as working with interior designers, decorators and architects. Fofana regularly travels to Paris, from where he connects with buyers and galleries.

Left: Aboubakar Fofana, mineral *bògòlanfini* cushion.

Above: Aboubakar Fofana, resist-stitch indigo cotton cushion stack.

Opposite: Aboubakar Fofana, indigo dyeing process.

Aïssa Dione Tissus

Senegal

A creator of West Africa's contemporary textile industry, Aïssa Dione's eponymous brand epitomizes African luxury. Aïssa Dione is renowned for her sophisticated textile collections that have attracted commissions from the likes of Hermès, Jacques Grange and Rose Tarlow.

'Aïssa Dione's innate artistic sense and design knowledge has given Mandjaque weaving an added nobility, brightness and opulence...propelling it to new heights of success as a textile for decoration and furniture upholstery.'

Aïssa Dione

Of French–Senegalese heritage, award-winning textile artist Aïssa Dione grew up in France, where she studied fine arts and began her career as a painter, moving to Senegal in her twenties to develop her art. It was in Senegal that she turned to textiles, having offered to help a client, who wanted to buy one of her paintings, redecorate his office. Her textiles were soon picked up by the local press and attracted the attention of a leading international designer, Christian Liaigre, who placed an order; others subsequently followed. The textiles are also used to make personal and home decor accessories, and cover her collection of beautifully crafted furniture.

In 1992, Aïssa Dione started a workshop working with one of the last remaining Mandjaque groups in Senegal and a single hand-weaving machine. Over 80 staff now work in her factory in Rufisque on the outskirts of Dakar, where traditional know-how is combined with modern techniques and technology. She has developed her own looms, adapted from those used for traditional weaving, and also uses modern ones. Aïssa Dione's textiles are adapted from the hand-woven textile traditions of the Mandjaque people who had emigrated to Senegal from Guinea-Bissau, bringing their weaving techniques with them. She helped rejuvenate the intricately woven textile, increasing the width to make it commercially viable, and developing contemporary patterns and sophisticated colour palettes. She also improved the quality of the raw materials traditionally used, working with natural, locally and regionally sourced materials. She introduced the use

146

Top: Aïssa Dione,
woven textiles.

Above left: Aïssa Dione,
Rouges, woven textiles.

Above right: Aïssa Dione,
Dogon, woven textiles.

of raffia, combining it with local cotton to give it a more luxurious quality. Aïssa Dione uses organic cotton handspun in Tambacunda, an area in the south of Senegal, and *kinaf*, a herb imported from Mali and Burkina Faso, whose long fibres that make it suitable for weaving the organic collection. For this specific collection, dyes are derived from natural sources and include mud collected in the dry season from the bottom of a lake north of Dakar as well as a variety of vegetation.

Aïssa Dione's expertise in the local textile industry has led to collaborations with many notable artists from around the world, including indigo dye master Aboubakar Fofana, with whom she created *sawura*,

an organic cotton dyed with natural indigo. Aïssa Dione's expertise has also been called upon by the governments of Burkina Faso and Togo to help develop and save their classical weaving cultures. She has helped introduce sophisticated designs, training, and improvements in quality, enabling the local weavers to respond to commercial requirements while maintaining the uniqueness of their cultures.

Below: Banke Kuku, green cushion from the Delta collection; inspired by the oil spills in the Niger Delta region of Nigeria.

Opposite: Banke Kuku, Pride fabric collection, presenting a young, modern Africa juxtaposed with design influences of the West; and wrapper fabric collections.

Banke Kuku

Nigeria · UK

Creating 'fashion for interiors', Banke Kuku is a London-based textiles designer whose work is a fusion of African and Western culture. Born in Nigeria, Kuku moved to the UK when she was eight, bringing with her the treasured memories of her birthplace.

Banke Kuku's eponymous company specializes in innovative printed and woven textiles inspired by a fusion of African and Western styles. Kuku's vibrant and intricately patterned designs are luxuriously opulent, drawing on the strengths of the cultures that influence them. She has designed for both fashion and interiors, and her fabrics are often paired with classic European furniture. Her love of bold patterns and colours that run the gamut from subtle to electric have earned her the sobriquet 'Queen of Colour'.

After graduating from Central Saint Martins and Chelsea College of Arts in London with a BA in textile design, Kuku announced her entry into the world of textile design with a collection of 'loud, vibrant and undeniably playful prints'. This marked the launch of a successful career in fashion, designing textiles that have been used in the collections of some of the world's leading designers, including Duro Olowu, Burberry and Jasmine di Milo, in addition to collaborating with some of the biggest names in African fashion such as Jewel by Lisa (now known as Lisa Folawiyo).

Kuku also uses her attention-grabbing designs to highlight social and environmental issues. In the Delta collection, her signature clashing colours and contrasting textures take the viewer on a visual journey through the effects of the devastating oil spills in Nigeria's Niger Delta oil fields.

'I have a love and obsession for textiles! I'm inspired by colour and patterns. They are very prominent in my work.'

Banke Kuku

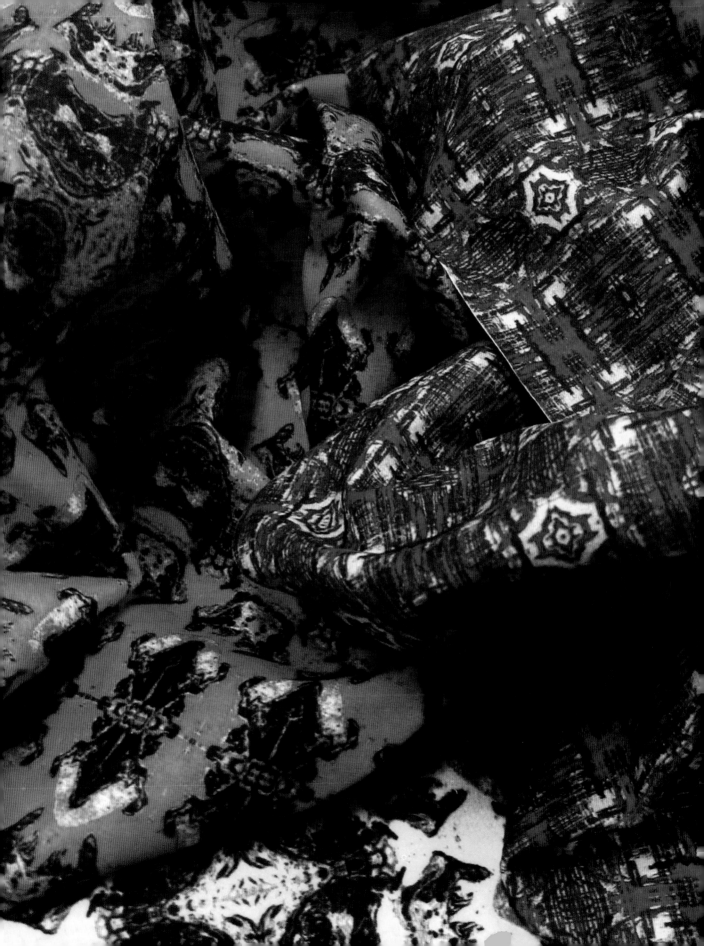

Below left: Banke Kuku, Lace Orchid
ottoman, influenced by the habitat of
the African moth, giving the print an
organic and botanic essence.

Below right: Banke Kuku, Delta
ottoman, inspired by the oil spills
in the Niger Delta region of Nigeria.

Opposite: Banke Kuku, Modern
Traditions collection cushions and
upholstery on black grandfather chair.

'I give a clear insight to those who
don't know the continent in its
modern and ever-evolving state.'

Banke Kuku

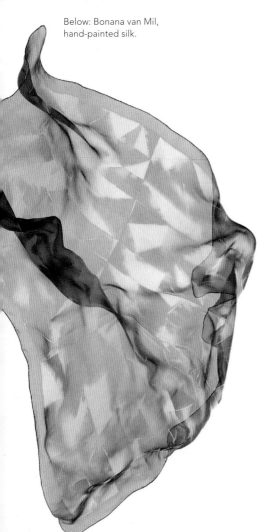

Bonana van Mil

Botswana · France

**Paris-based textile designer Bonana van Mil describes her work
as storytelling using colours and motifs rather than text to convey
her emotions and inspirations. Van Mil is inspired by Africa's
dying traditions – fabrics, storytelling and ceremonies – along
with souvenirs and vivid mental images from her travels, and
constantlyrecalls the precious memories of her childhood
growing up in Africa.**

Born in Botswana, van Mil moved to the Netherlands with her family
when she was young and she spent her teenage years divided between
Botswana, Zimbabwe and the Netherlands. A love of fine arts led her to
a local art school where she studied the subject for a year, leaving after
receiving encouragement from her tutor to look into applied arts. She
later studied fashion design at the Utrecht Graduate School of Visual
Art and Design in the Netherlands, followed by an MA in design at
the University of Utrecht. Van Mil settled in Paris in 2008, drawn to
the inspirational city of fashion, love and culture, and she debuted her
eponymous accessories label in 2011.

This continuous movement has had a profound effect on her work, which
she defines as being a mix between two completely opposite cultures.
Van Mil's designs see chaos and order fighting each other for dominance,
representing the clash of cultures between Africa, with its shimmering
colours and chaotic structures, and Europe, with its rigid organization
and minimalism. The result is a modern, edgy take on techniques such as
tie-dye, whereby hard, jagged geometric lines are softened by the blurring
effect of the colours bleeding into each other. These effects are achieved
by hand-painting the designs onto pure silk or wool and silk blends. Van
Mil is also drawn to the hand-craftsmanship used in traditional textiles
around the world, and seeks to understand and translate these techniques
into her own work. She constantly experiments with techniques such as
dyeing, weaving and embroidery to create new fabrics.

Van Mil's textiles cross the boundaries between fashion and interiors,
areas she continues to explore.

'My work describes
mostly little memories
of places I have visited.
What was... at those
moments normal
and obvious [is] now
precious and inspiring.'

Bonana van Mil

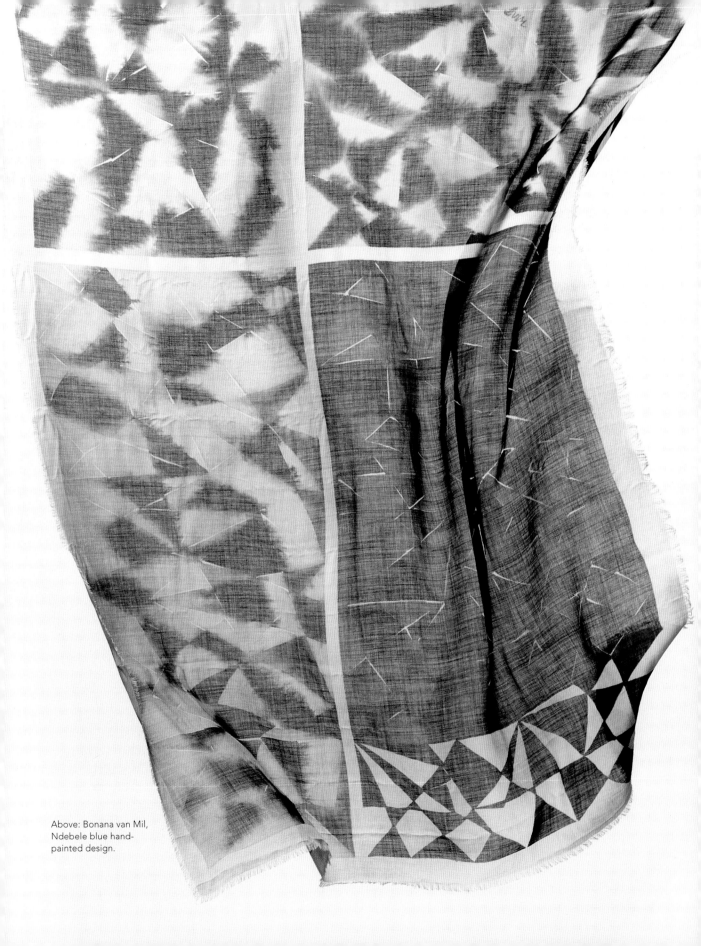

Above: Bonana van Mil, Ndebele blue hand-painted design.

Dar Leone

Sierra Leone · UK

Dar Leone, a textiles and interior accessories brand, is infused with the laid-back sophistication of the global traveller. The company was founded in 2012 by Isatu Funna, a US attorney of Sierra Leonian heritage, who lives in London.

> 'I wanted to be surrounded by the Africa that I grew up in and could not find pictured anywhere.'
>
> *Isatu Funna*

For Funna, Dar Leone is the fulfilment of a long-held interest in African interior design and a wider passion for global design and cultures. Dar Leone celebrates the diversity of cultures by actively seeking out the individual expressions of beauty, craftsmanship and style that come with tradition and heritage, and was a way for Funna to bring her brand of 'global traveller style' into the home. The name Dar Leone embodies the fusing of cultures to create something new, and serves to incorporate Funna's multicultural upbringing and experiences.

Funna started outsourcing decorative objects akin to the treasured finds brought back from idyllic holidays to far-flung destinations, but, as she explains, an underlying desire to be surrounded by the Africa of her memories led her to create her own designs, starting with textiles. Designed and handmade in London, Dar Leone's debut textile and soft furnishings collections launched in 2013. The textiles are a reflection of Funna's Sierra Leonian heritage, harking back to a 'childhood spent in the sunnier climes of Freetown and in Côte d'Ivoire.'

Dar Leone's textiles pay homage to West Africa's creative past and maritime culture. Motifs based on antique gold filigree are used to invoke memories of Africa's ancient kingdoms. Africa's textile histories are present in Dar Leone's sourced collections, which include Sierra Leone's 'country cloth' and Congolese kuba cloth. Classical textiles are also hinted at in Dar Leone's own designs: West Africa's renowned strip-weaving techniques can be seen in the Tropic Marine collection, reinterpreted through the use of modern techniques such as digital printing onto heavy linens and cottons.

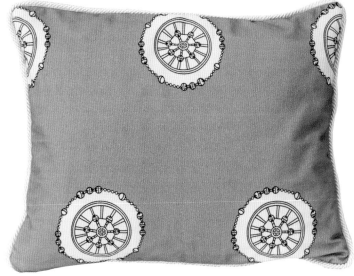

Above: Dar Leone, Tropic Marine fabric, lush diamond and stripes inspired by the traditional textiles of Sierra Leone.

Right: Dar Leone, Manua boudoir pillow, inspired by the Atlantic and antique Ghanaian gold.

Opposite: Dar Leone, Tropic Marine collection, Dea Hots floor cushion.

Design Maketo
DRC · UK

Textile designer Henoc Maketo draws inspiration from the vibrant printed textiles of his home country, the Democratic Republic of Congo (DRC); they are reflected in the multi-layered motifs and rich vibrant colour palettes that make up his designs.

'Since I can remember in my childhood with my friends, I was always drawing on the ground, freehand with a stick – any subject as a test. Often, my drawings were most perfect.'

Henoc Maketo

Specializing in screen-printing, Maketo employs traditional and modern print techniques to produce his designs. He favours freehand drawing over computer-aided design (CAD), which he uses to finalize the digitally printed designs. In 1975, a friend who saw his potential enrolled Maketo on an art course at the Académie des Beaux-Arts in Kinshasa, DRC. He subsequently studied graphic design, working for a local studio before moving to a textile company where he designed dress fabrics. This came to an end in 1991 when political turmoil in the DRC saw the closure of many local companies. With no job, Maketo opened his own graphic design studio, Design Maketo. In 1995, he was invited to participate in 'Next Generation', a series of conferences and workshops at ICOGRADA in Solothurn, Switzerland. This opportunity enabled Maketo to build on his screen-printing skills, in addition to being introduced to CAD. The worsening situation in his country meant that a few years later Maketo was forced to shut his studio and he migrated to the UK in 1999.

Maketo set about rebuilding his design career and after a long, hard road returned to university in 2007 and earned a BA in printed textile design from the University of East London. A few months after graduating, Maketo won the New Design Britain, Fabrics award at *Interiors Birmingham* 2011. The award brought with it a placement at ercol, the British furniture company, who presented the textiles he created for their iconic furniture at *Tent London*. Although Maketo sees himself as a fashion fabrics designer, his experience brought about an interest in creating textiles for furniture and interiors. That said, for Maketo winning the award ultimately meant one thing – going to back to being a designer. He has since taken his designs home to the DRC and is helping to reignite the dialogue towards rebuilding the local textile and fashion design industries. Although Maketo works alone, he has started to work with his son who is following in his father's footsteps by studying graphic design.

'After being awarded
the New Design Britain,
Fabrics award in 2011,
I could go back to always
working as a designer.'

Henoc Maketo

Above: Henoc Maketo, Ercol studio
couch and backdrop in Henoc Maketo
marble fruits fabric.

Right: Henoc Maketo, Ercol evergreen
two-seater sofa in Henoc Maketo
marble fruits fabric.

Eva Sonaike

Nigeria · UK

'The intensity in colours, clothing, nature, street-scenes, and architecture – everything is so vibrant and intense in this part of the world and gives me such a great scope of inspiration.'

Eva Sonaike

'Bringing colour to life' is the mission of Eva Sonaike, a London-based company specializing in luxury West African-inspired textiles, home decor and accessories.

The brand was set up in 2009 by Eva Sonaike, who came to design via a career as a journalist; she was a fashion editor for *Elle* magazine. 'I was on maternity leave with my first child and wanted to redecorate the house,' she says. 'I couldn't find any cushions and textiles that inspired me. So I decided to make my own.' Encouraged by the response, her brand developed. Sonaike's quest was to bring her passion for African fabrics and her exuberant love for colour to the high-end market and in doing so explore the notion of 'African luxury'. Eva Sonaike became the first home textiles company to reinterpret the ever-popular *ankara* (wax cloth) fabrics, introducing them to the high-end interiors market through a range of distinctive signature designs, which deliver vibrancy and colour into people's lives.

Sonaike, who was born and raised in South Germany and is of Nigerian heritage, has taken the best elements of those cultures as inspiration for her work. Sonaike's designs draw from two distinct influences: Africa's affinity for colourful clothing, particularly the significance cloth has within West African culture both as a mark of identity and as gifts, and European antique and mid-century furniture traditions, assembled with the precision of German craftsmanship.

A self-confessed perfectionist, Sonaike sources the very best in finishing and fittings to complete her products, and places an emphasis on the finer details, from hand-finishing and high quality manufacturing down to the zips and hardware used. In a bid to control and oversee production, all Eva Sonaike textiles are printed in Germany, with product manufacturing carried out in England. Sonaike has also worked with weavers in Nigeria to produce traditional fabrics such as the Yoruba's *aso oke*, a vibrant woven cloth often reserved for special occasions such as weddings and religious festivals.

'The continent of Africa
first and foremost
inspires my work.
And in my case, West
Africa (Nigeria, Ghana,
Benin) – the places
that I visit regularly.'

Eva Sonaike

Julie Kouamo

Cameroon · France · UK

**Textile print designer Julie Kouamo's evocative fabric and wallpaper
designs feature a collage of multi-layered patterns, textures and
images. The designer, who launched her debut collection in 2008,
is greatly influenced by her heritage: her richly layered visual
narratives convey stories about her Cameroonian origins and
French upbringing.**

Julie Kouamo studied art in Paris and subsequently graduated from
London's Central Saint Martins with a degree in textile design; she
specialized in print. Hand-printed, hand-dyed or digitally printed,
Julie Kouamo designs are produced in the UK, where she is based, and
range from bold arabesque motifs to delicate depictions of nature and
cultural symbolism. Her sources of inspiration are many, ranging from
her travels and art to everyday life and her African heritage, 'Cameroon
is a great source of inspiration,' she says, 'the colours, the vegetation, the
textiles...will always translate through my work.'

She feels a strong affinity to nature, in particular vegetation, and looks
to things such as the individual patterns in leaves and the adverse effects
of weather on man-made objects. This is a defining characteristic of
her work. 'It is amazing how clever nature is,' she says, 'and I think a lot
of patterns already exist in nature. I love looking closely at vegetation
and try to reproduce through textiles and techniques what nature has
created.' She experiments with a wide range of classic techniques from
Europe, Africa and Asia, including linocut, screen-printing, batik, block
printing, foiling, flocking, over-printing, rusting and dip dyeing, as well as
modern techniques such as computer manipulation and advanced digital
technology. Her distinctive style also involves researching photography
and drawing techniques, which are applied to form the patterns.

'I want to tell my story
through my prints,
but I aim as well to
inspire and get people
to travel with them.'

Julie Kouamo

Below: Julie Kouamo,
Nenta chair.

'I play a lot with traditional techniques like batik, resist-dyeing, block printing with screen-printing and manipulation through computers. My speciality would be to learn and understand techniques used by many cultures and to make it my own.'

Julie Kouamo

Below left: Julie Kouamo,
'Brooklyn Bridge' collection,
NYC Brooklyn padlock cushion.

Right: Julie Kouamo.
Bami chair, exotic vine wallpaper.

Bottom: Julie Kouamo.
Bangou collection, cushions.

Le Ndomo

Mali

In 2008, textile designer and art teacher Boubacar Doumbia set up Le Ndomo, a social enterprise, with the aim of addressing the issues relating to youth unemployment in his home country of Mali. Operating from a workshop based in Ségou, Mali's third largest city, Le Ndomo produces richly patterned fabrics using natural dyes on 100% organic cotton.

'For inspiration,
I refer to the traditional
designs of the soil.'

Boubacar Doumbia

Doumbia had always liked graphic art since he was a child, and studied fine arts, graduating from Mali's National Institute of the Arts (INA). Doumbia is part of an association of painters called the Kasobané Group, whose priority is to use classical techniques. Following a long-held interest in Mali's classical textile-making techniques, Doumbia has conducted extensive research into textile techniques and the use of natural vegetable dyes. Le Ndomo makes use of classical strip-weaving methods, in addition to using contemporary looms to produce wider fabric lengths, which are then dyed or decorated using centuries-old methods such as *bògòlanfini* (mud cloth) and appliqué. The fabrics are then used to produce locally and internationally sold home furnishings and personal accessories. Placing an emphasis on the quality of craftsmanship and attention to detail, all the work produced at Le Ndomo is done by hand – from the spinning and weaving to decorating. Le Ndomo also offers workshops and lecturers upon request for those wanting to learn more about the art of natural dyes and traditional textile production.

Through Le Ndomo, Doumbia embodies the philosophy of teaching young people a technical skill, training those taking part in the programme with the local knowledge of textile production. Doumbia, however, does more than just provide technical training and strives to instil the values of traditional African society in the young apprentices. The students

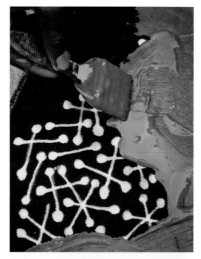

'Contemporary design
from Africa can offer
the world a new vision
of modern Africa with
shapes and patterns
inspired by African
cultural heritage.'

Boubacar Doumbia

are taught essential life skills to help them become responsible, self-sufficient adults and are encouraged to strive for personal development through the enhancement of personal values such as responsibility, commitment and teamwork towards achieving their desired goals. They are also taught the skills they might need one day to set up and run their own businesses.

Doumbia occasionally collaborates with other designers to create new designs and in September 2013, as part of the Design Network Africa programme, of which he is a member, he collaborated with Habitat UK to design a range of sustainably produced *bògòlanfini*-based soft furnishings, using natural dyes and river mud. The designs featured intricate patterns in deep, rich hues.

Mariem Besbes

Tunisia

Dancer turned textile designer Mariem Besbes is an expert in hand-mixing the exquisite natural colours that characterize her textile collections. From her atelier, Besbes explores Tunisia's rich textile heritage, for instance the deep-hued purple cheesecloth fabrics worn by the ancient Romans. In the process she has revived many forgotten natural dye techniques.

'For me, vegetal colours are like small stories. Stories which send me towards a memory or something we know from the past and is universal.'

Mariem Besbes
(Selvedge, Issue 17)

Born in Carthage, Tunisia, Besbes grew up in Paris, where she studied contemporary dance under the tutelage of Dominique Dupuy, co-founder of the Ballet modernes de Paris. Besbes later attended the Duperré School of Applied Arts in Paris and studied textile design. Returning to Tunisia, she began working with textiles, opening her atelier in an old converted barn in Tunis. Here Besbes has spent endless hours experimenting with weaving and dyeing cloths: growing plants, grinding, kneading and sifting them to mix her own colour palettes, which included crimson reds, purples, and variants on yellow saffron, ochre and sienna. Besbes sought out elderly women in the community who had knowledge of Tunisia's natural dye traditions and, while speaking to some elderly silk-weavers, learnt that her grandfather was a pioneering silk-weaver who had left Tunisia in the 1910s for Lyons to learn about silk-weaving manufacturing techniques, introducing the foundations of modern weaving to Tunisia.

Besbes also draws inspiration from the *haik*, a traditional Tunisian cloth comprised of a large, heavy oblong shape worn around the body which is transparent from the inside. The fabric is ideal for use as soft furnishings such as curtains, as it lets in light while preventing anyone outside from seeing what is happening inside. Besbes uses locally sourced wool, which is washed, spun and woven by hand, a process that changes the fibre from rough to smooth and delicate, creating a type of wool gauze.

Besbes's expertise has led to a number of notable collaborations. Between 2005 and 2009 she collaborated with Hermès, creating unique pieces for brand showcases. In 2008, Besbes's knowledge of ancient plant dyes led her to create collections for trend forecaster Li Edelkoort Studio in Paris. In the same year she worked alongside costume designer Chloe Obolensky creating costumes for the theatre production *Berenice* at the Théâtre des Bouffes du Nord in Paris. Besbes has also worked with UNESCO and with local NGOs to create Eos, an association of female artisans in rural areas, with the aim of using local knowledge and skills to improve their livelihoods. Besbes has also designed exclusive collections for several luxury hospitality properties, including hand-woven carpets for the suites of Villa Didon Carthage and high-end retailers such as The Conran Shop.

Petel

Mauritania · USA

Petel was created in 2012 by Ibrahima and Julie Wagne, who, inspired by the beautiful textiles of Mauritania, sought to share them with the world by creating a range of personal and interior accessories. The couple met in 2000 while working with the Peace Corps in Mauritania and now live in San Francisco.

> 'I've always found the technique of tying strings to a wooden tree loom a fascinating and meticulously wonderful way of creating something gorgeous out of nothing.'
>
> *Ibrahima Wagne*

Ibrahima grew up in the village of Boghé in Mauritania and maintains strong connections to his heritage. Mauritania's textiles have played a significant role in his life and he recalls how his 'mother gifted Julie one of her blankets when we got engaged, as well as when our first daughter was born.' The Wagnes have built relationships with some of the local Fulani weavers, working with them to source or create the textiles used in Petel's collections, which combine West African colours and patterns with a contemporary Western aesthetic.

The textiles, whether vintage or newly woven, are unique to the Fulani tribe. They are hand-woven by master weavers using nothing but string and rugged, handmade tree looms in a tradition that has been passed on from father to son, generation to generation. 'It is truly an artform,' they say, 'and it still exists today because the weavers have a deep-rooted sense of tradition and respect for the craft.' Like many of the continent's textile traditions, Fulani textiles are a cultural identity marker, mainly used for ceremonial occasions. Fulani women also use the textiles as decorative accessories; the fabrics are often one of the most expensive pieces they own.

Opposite: Petel,
leather tag detail.

Above: Petel, hand-
woven Fulani textiles.

177

Noting that the tradition of hand-weaving is a dying art in Mauritania, the couple wanted to support the weavers, not only by using the textiles they create, but also by using Petel's profits to create a training programme for younger Fulani artists interested in learning weaving from older weavers. 'If the younger generation of Fulani see ancillary value in their traditional textiles, the methods will be preserved.' This ethos inspired the company's name: petel means 'little spark' in Pulaar, the language of the weavers, and as the couple say, 'It is our dream that this "little spark" will ignite a fire of hope, inspiration and self-sufficiency among the Fulani weavers in Mauritania.' Part of the reluctance to take up the craft is because the weaving process is painstakingly laborious and repetitive, taking between three and four weeks to make a complete unit of fabric.

'We believe that through Petel we can reinvest in the vibrant colour and culture from the land that brought us together by introducing these traditional handmade textiles to a broader audience.'

Julie Wagne

Below: Ronél Jordaan, pebble pillow, hand-felted merino wool, Snob.

Opposite: Ronél Jordaan, pebble strands, silk and wool circle cushion, leaf-cut recycled-wool rug, boulder Ndebele chair, hand-felted merino wool, Amaridian.

Ronél Jordaan Textiles

South Africa

'My designs are simple or complicated. It is dictated by the idea or concept.'

Ronél Jordaan

The owner of a pioneering handmade felt factory in Johannesburg, South Africa, Ronél Jordaan is one of the country's leading textile artists. Inspired by nature and its organic forms and textures, Jordaan seeks to bring the beauty, purity and tranquillity of nature into the home through her designs, and in the process elevate the craft of feltmaking to a contemporary artform.

Jordaan initially studied drama at the University of Pretoria and was introduced to textile printing by a friend. Drawn to the discipline, she changed direction to pursue a career in textile design instead. Jordaan started her career in 1977 when she began working as a designer at a local textile factory. Self-taught in the art of feltmaking, it was on an art therapy course between 2001 and 2002 that she began working and experimenting with the material.

Ever conscious of the environment, Jordaan takes care to ensure her products not only look good, but are also good for overall wellbeing. This respect for the environment is translated through the use of eco-friendly processes and natural materials. Ronél Jordaan products are made from 100% South African merino wool that is free of harmful irritating acids commonly used in wool-treating processes. The wool is dyed with natural dyes and certified as lead free. Featured in her original felted wool collection, life-like rocks and pebbles have become Jordaan's signature products, complemented by a range of furnishings and personal accessories.

The art of felting is not a traditional South African craft, but in a conscious effort to alleviate unemployment among women living in the city's townships, Jordaan began training and working with local women in the craft. Her company, which employs mostly women, remains dedicated

Below: Ronél Jordaan, boulders, rocks, pebbles, hand-felted merino wool.

Opposite, clockwise from the top: Ronél Jordaan, Ndebele poufs, daisy stool and dreadlock cushions, Amaridian; all hand-felted merino wool.

'I am the owner of a handmade felt factory... This gives me the ability to do product development a lot faster as there is no design dilution through conversation.'

Ronél Jordaan

to transferring skills. Depending on the designs to be produced, Jordaan also utilizes the skills of street crafters, whether it's wet felting, weaving, knitting or any other appropriate techniques that she feels will suit the design concept. Ronél Jordaan is a member of Design Network Africa.

Sabahar

Ethiopia

The Sabahar Silk Garden in Addis Ababa, Ethiopia, is a place that promotes and celebrates the artistry and heritage of Ethiopia's longstanding weaving traditions. The word 'saba' refers to the Queen of Sheba, while 'har' is the Amharic word for silk, hence 'Sabahar'. Sabahar work with weavers from around the country to design and produce contemporary collections of luxurious hand-woven silk and cotton home and fashion accessories.

'Our products are unique within the Ethiopian context in various ways. Probably our most special aspect is that we are the only company [currently] producing and using Ethiopian "Eri" silk.'

Kathy Marshall

Sabahar was established in 2006 by Kathy Marshall, a Canadian who moved to Ethiopia in 1994 with the aim of creating a sustainable business that would help create employment opportunities and enable sustainable income; all while being globally competitive and profitable. 'I believed (and still do!) that there was an opportunity in the global market for well-made, unique Ethiopian textiles,' Marshall says. Weaving in Ethiopia dates back to ancient times, but some of the techniques are in danger of dying out in favour of modern, often imported products. All Sabahar's products are hand-woven on traditional looms using age-old skills passed down through the generations. Sabahar has a staff of about 55 and outsources to over 100 spinners and weavers, who work from home or through cooperatives. Sabahar also collaborates with local and international designers, who work closely with the weavers to produce classic and contemporary designs.

With the exception of a percentage of the silk cocoons used, every aspect of Sabahar's production process is local, from the silk cocoons raised by and then bought from farmers, to the spinning, weaving and dyeing. Weaving with imported synthetic fibres has been practised in Ethiopia over the centuries, but silk is relatively new to Ethiopia. Eri silk, which is produced in Ethiopia, has a linen-like texture, unlike Mulberry silk, which is also used, and has the more finely woven, shiny texture commonly associated with silk. All the silk is sourced from both Ethiopia and India. Sabahar also works with Ethiopian cotton, which is hand-spun and dyed using low impact dyes. The dyes used for the silks are locally sourced and 100% natural, although purchased dyes are also used. Sabahar is a member of Design Network Africa and the World Fair Trade Organization.

Shine Shine

South Africa

'I've been fascinated and inspired by African design my whole life, and the medium that captures the spirit and expression of Africa most vividly is textile design... It makes me happy to bring this contemporary take on an age-old pan-African custom into being.'

Tracy Rushmere

Playful, colourful, funky and feisty, brimming with attitude and urban glamour, Shine Shine, a Cape Town-based textile company, is creating a new version of the ever-popular 'African fabric and prints' for the young – and young at heart.

Shine Shine was founded in 2007 by South African entrepreneur Tracy Rushmere. Her long interest in textiles, in particular the political, religious and commemorative cloths popular across the continent, provided the inspiration to create a more contemporary textile, one that celebrated urban African culture and captured the pulsating energy of a young and vibrant continent. Having travelled widely across the continent, Rushmere had observed the African approach to wearing and interacting with cloth: 'Africa has a way of doing things,' she notes, 'things have different values here.' As with the fabrics that inspire them, storytelling is at the heart of all Shine Shine's fabrics.

Rushmere is also drawn to beautiful yet quirky things, an interest that is translated into the Shine Shine aesthetic, which is filled with the tongue-in-cheek humour of a cool urban Africa. Shine Shine's distinctive visual aesthetic is the result of a creative partnership between Rushmere and fellow South African graphic designer Heidi Chisholm. Imagined by Chisholm and brought to life by Rushmere, their textile collaborations began when they worked together for a local brand called Afro Coffee. They have successfully forged what Rushmere describes as 'a nice partnership', saying 'we speak the same language.' Both are inspired by and drawn to similar points of reference, as, for example, with the painted barber shop signs seen across the continent.

In 2000, Chisholm co-founded the design studio Daddy Buy Me a Pony in Cape Town, starting a magazine called Afro with the aim of inspiring 'South African designers to look at Africa as their inspiration instead of looking at Western

Below: Shine Shine,
O'Baby orange cushon.

Opposite: Shine Shine,
Julie Juu and Jennifer
Paris textiles.

design books. We wanted Africans to make heroes of
their own artists and musicians. We also wanted the
world to see the cool things that were happening in
Africa.' As a natural extension of her graphic design
work, Chisholm began designing textiles in 2006. In
2008, she moved to Brooklyn, New York, where she set
up her eponymous design studio. Despite the distance,
the Heidi–Tracy partnership continues to thrive.

Shine Shine's fabrics are translated into a range
of clothing, personal and interior accessories and
upholstery, as well as into non-fabric-based products.
They all attract a local and international clientele.

'With each of the fabrics, I try
to tell a story. The stories are
really simple, everyday life, about
contemporary, urban Africa,
but they are also universal.'

Heidi Chisholm

Below: Skinny laMinx,
bird in flight print.

Skinny laMinx
South Africa

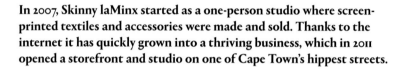

In 2007, Skinny laMinx started as a one-person studio where screen-printed textiles and accessories were made and sold. Thanks to the internet it has quickly grown into a thriving business, which in 2011 opened a storefront and studio on one of Cape Town's hippest streets.

Founded by South African illustrator and designer Heather Moore, Skinny laMinx grew out of a hobby. Moore loves producing hand-drawn illustrations and creating papercut silhouettes that often make their way into the textiles used to create the business's ever-increasing product range. Moore's designs are rendered in fresh colour palettes, the whimsical simplicity of the designs drawing on and fusing a range of influences from South Africa to Scandinavia. Her inspiration comes from all around, with random moments such as the simple act of opening a packet of salad leading to a new fabric design featuring lettuce leaves, or the roaming herds, based on a 2000-year-old cave drawing, which made their way onto a cushion cover.

Working from a studio above her shop, Moore is essentially self-taught and has learnt the business of design as she has gone along. 'I was itching to make things that I liked, just for fun,' she says. 'It turned out that people liked these things I was making, and so I became better at it.' Moore trained as a Drama and English teacher, working in educational illustration and later comic scriptwriting for about 10 years before setting up a studio armed with a silkscreen. Blogging about her work from the start helped Moore gain an international following and Skinny laMinx's textiles and products can now be found in stores and homes around the globe.

Skinny laMinx is a proudly South African company and, despite achieving international success, Moore has deliberately chosen to keep the company small and resolutely local, resisting the pressures to carry out production somewhere cheaper. All the designing and manufacturing happens locally and uses cotton milled in Cape Town.

'My designs draw on my environment and experience – both global and local – resulting in a clean, simple, Scandi-tinged design aesthetic that's also perfectly at home in Africa.'

Heather Moore

Above: Skinny laMinx,
Afro-Scandi backdrop
and cushion pile.

Right and far right: Skinny
laMinx, pebble and rough
diamond cushions.

Overleaf: Skinny laMinx,
soft bucket collection.

Tensira

Guinea · France

Husband and wife team Hamidou Diallo and Tuulia Makinen combined their backgrounds in business and fashion marketing to create Tensira, a home linens and accessories brand based on the weaving and textile traditions of Guinea.

'From my first journey in Africa, I was captured by the beauty of African fabrics... They are fabrics of wellbeing, totally ecological, and their fibres are filled with history.'

Tuulia Makinen

Tensira, which has headquarters in Paris, was launched in 2010. It was inspired by a visit to Diallo's home country of Guinea, where Makinen fell in love with the local crafts, fabrics, stripes and indigos, which gave them the idea of transforming these traditional crafts into modern home linen and accessories. Diallo was aware that the local crafts would disappear if efforts were not made to keep them alive, so he wanted to introduce the textile traditions of his homeland to a wider audience, and Tensira was the platform that allowed him to achieve this goal.

Makinen is Tensira's artistic director, designing the textile collections for the soft furnishings and personal accessories. She draws inspiration from her father, who was an architect and instilled in her a passion for design, and also from her mother-in-law, who has been a multi-talented indigo dyer for more than 40 years. Originally from Finland, Makinen came to Paris in 2005 to study, working in luxury fashion before turning to textile design.

Tensira produces two collections a year, for spring/summer and fall/winter. The textiles are centred on Guinea's traditional stripe and check patterns, and are created in Tensira's two Guinea-based workshops, the second of which opened in 2013. The company works directly with highly skilled artisans who specialize in weaving, sewing and dyeing. The textiles are made from 100% cotton and are hand-woven on traditional looms. The indigos are dyed with vegetable indigo dye, in a process that is carried out in villages situated in Guinea's mountain region. Tensira also experiments with the ancient techniques and launched a new light, plain indigo in 2014. Tensira's product range extends to terracotta pottery and wooden furniture, all produced in partnership with West African artisans. Along with a showroom in Paris, Tensira's products are carried by more than 100 retailers in 18 countries across the globe.

Top left: Tensira, vegetal indigo-dyed textiles, 100% hand-woven cotton.

Above left: Tensira, striped *kas* textiles, 100% hand-woven cotton.

Top right: Tensira, table linen, 100% hand-woven cotton.

Above right: Tensira, throws and bedcover with fringing, 100% hand-woven cotton.

Yéleen Design

Mali · France

Yéleen Design was founded in 2003 by Aïda Duplessis, a Malian textile designer. Based between Bamako and Paris, Duplessis initially started working in tourism, having studied history of art and tourism. She left it behind after a brief stint to concentrate on raising her family.

'In my heart I have always been a designer, I have always tried to redesign and adapt African arts in a modern way; to make them more comfortable.'

Aïda Duplessis

During this period Duplessis began to experiment with creating her own textiles, beginning with beautiful table linens inspired by her Malian heritage. 'People were so impressed by the concept, the traditional textiles and raw materials I used,' she says 'that I decided to create my own.' Raised by her grandmother, Duplessis recalls her using the fragrant roots of the vetiver to scent water and make incense (vetiver is a perennial grass that has long been used by Malian women to create perfumes). The memory of this sparked Duplessis's idea of weaving with the grass to create rugs and mats. Duplessis also experiments with other natural and organic fibres such as cotton, flax, hemp and nettle.

Learning as she went along, Duplessis travelled extensively, researching fibres from around the world and seeking other materials that would complement them. Having gathered the necessary knowledge, Duplessis sought to combine Mali's age-old hand-weaving techniques with innovative applications of the fibres. Setting up her workshop in Bamako, Mali's capital city, Duplessis began working with local spinners, who were women, and weavers, who were men, to create new, modern textile designs that are translated into a range of home furnishings collections for both interior and exterior use.

Duplessis's textiles are inextricably linked to nature, and as such she upholds a commitment to promoting ethical awareness and sustainability. Yéleen Design currently has a staff of 20, who are regularly offered training to help with improving and developing their handwork techniques, as well as instilling the value of understanding the meaning of quality. Duplessis works with decorators, architects and retailers to develop her unique textiles, which can be found around the world.

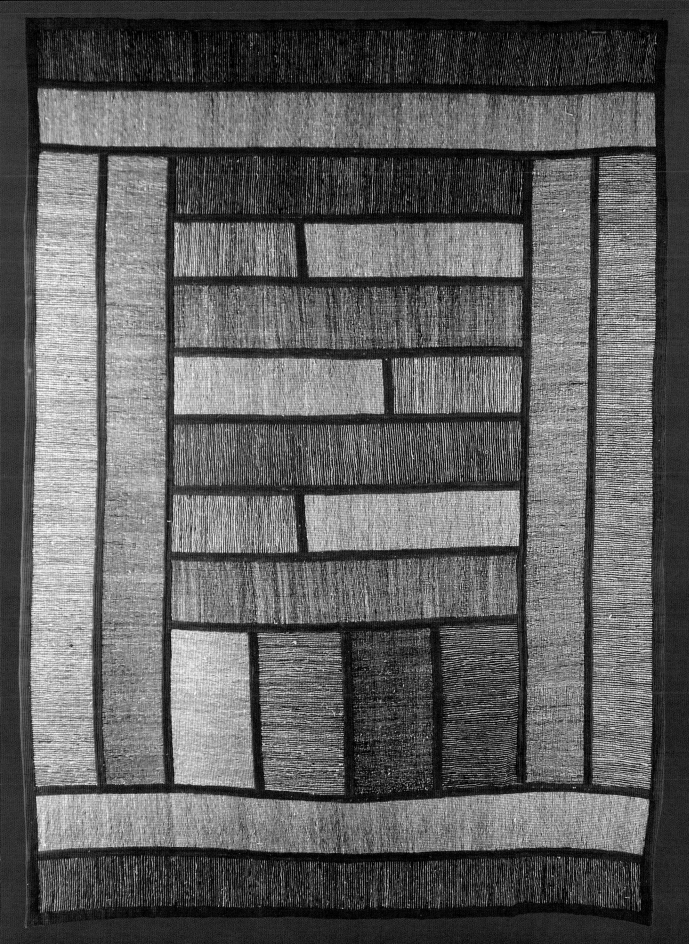

'All textile fibres inspire me...
all textures, all colours, all forms.'

Aïda Duplessis

Opposite: Yéleen Design,
textile (detail).

Top: Yéleen Design,
Argentik collection, cushions.

Above left: Yéleen Design,
hemp cushions.

Above right: Yéleen Design,
woven carpet with red edging.

Yemi Awosile

Nigeria · UK

'I'm interested in the aesthetic value of materials in relation to people and spaces. My aim is to develop projects which promote creative dialogue between international borders.'

Yemi Awosile

London-based designer Yemi Awosile produces materials and textiles for objects and spaces. She works in collaboration with manufacturers, designers and visual artists, sometimes to commission. Awosile started her creative practice in 2008 with the aim of developing projects that promote a creative dialogue across international borders.

Awosile is motivated by the process of gathering information about raw materials in their natural state and then relating the materials' aesthetic value to people and places on an everyday level.

In 2014, Awosile developed a new body of work as part of the UNESCO *Bark Cloth in Architecture, Arts and Design* show, which was exhibited at IMM Cologne in Germany. Awosile produced *The Mutuba Project*, a range of lighting made from bark cloth, which is cultivated by small-scale organic farmers in Uganda. She worked very closely on the project with a Ugandan–German family business who are pioneers in the production of bark cloth fabric. Other projects developed by Awosile have included exploring alternative applications for post-consumer waste from the cork industry. She examined the naturally inherent properties in cork and was particularly interested in cork's thermal and acoustic insulating properties, transferring her findings to textile collections and products aimed at interior architectural applications.

In addition to her studio work, Awosile also designs and facilitates workshops aimed at the wider public and fellow creative practitioners. Her past collaborators have included the Crafts Council and the British Council, and, in London, the Victoria and Albert Museum, the Tate and the Southbank Centre. Awosile has also held visiting teaching posts at Loughborough University, Chelsea College of Arts, London, and the London College of Fashion. Awosile herself studied textile design in London at Chelsea College of Arts and at the Royal College of Art where she graduated with an MA in constructed textiles.

Opposite, above and right: Yemi Awosile, *The Mutuba Project*, 2014. Lighting made using bark cloth, a natural material from Uganda obtained from the permanently renewable bark of the East African fig tree, known locally as the mutuba tree. The bark is harvested every year without felling the tree, and has a distinctive and natural fibre structure resembling hand-woven bast fibre.

Glossary

Adinkra symbols A form of visual communication used by the Asante, which dates back hundreds of years.

Amhara People of Ethiopia's central highlands.

Asante People of South-Central Ghana, parts of Côte d'Ivoire and Togo.

Baganda People of the ancient Buganda Kingdom, which was a centralized state in South Uganda.

Bamana (also Bambara) People of Mali's central regions.

Bamun (also Bamum) People of Cameroon's southwest grassland regions.

bark cloth A natural textile created from the bark of certain trees, which is beaten, felted and dyed.

Baule People of Côte d'Ivoire.

Benin The Kingdom of a powerful and wealthy West African kingdom, in the Edo state, thought to have been founded in the 13th century. Now located in southwest Nigeria.

Benin Bronzes The collective term given to over 1,000 works of art dating back to the 13th century, which were created in the royal palace of the Kingdom of Benin. Not all of the pieces were bronze.

Dogon People of Mali in West Africa.

Dorze People of the Gamo Highlands in the Omo Valley of southern Ethiopia.

Ewe People of southern Togo, southeastern Ghana and southern Benin.

felting A highly skilled craft where threads of pure wool are rubbed together to build up the layers, a process that interlocks the follicles of the individual strands, which enables them to become matted and dense, giving felt its distinctive texture.

filigree A process by which delicate ornamental designs are created through the twisting, shaping and soldering of fine, thread-like wires, usually from precious metals. Filigree was introduced to North Africa by Jewish gold- and silversmiths settling in the region following the Spanish Inquisition in the 15th century. This was a turbulent period of history that saw the expulsion of Muslims and Jews.

Fulani Historically nomadic people of West Africa.

gudza A textile made from twisted fibres, taken from a tree's inner bark. Boiled in water to soften it, the fibre is then pounded with a type of pestle and mortar before being hand-rolled into lengths, which are dyed and then woven by hand.

Harar A walled city in eastern Ethiopia inhabited by the Harari people.

Himba Peoples of northern Namibia. Indigo Natural dye with a distinctive blue colour that was traditionally extracted from plants. In recent times, synthetic indigo dye has been used as a substitute.

indigo Natural dye with a distinctive blue colour that was traditionally extracted from plants. In recent times, synthetic indigo dye has been used as a substitute.

lost wax Method A means of shaping metal whereby a clay or plaster mould of the object is made and covered in wax. A second layer of clay is added and the mould is heated to melt the wax before molten metal is poured into the cavity. Once cooled and hardened, the clay is removed, leaving behind the shaped metal object.

Maasai (also Masai) Semi-nomadic peoples of southern Kenya and northern Tanzania.

Mandjaque (also Manjack) People of Guinea-Bissau, who also emigrated to Senegal.

mesob Lidded Ethiopian basket that also serves as a table.

Moshoeshoe I Founding father of Lesotho, who united several small Southern Sotho clans to establish the Basotho nation.

Ndebele a) South Ndebele peoples of South Africa; b) North Ndebele peoples of southern Zimbabwe.

sadza A thick porridge made from pounded maize.

Sahel The semi-arid area dividing the Sahara Desert and rainforest regions of Africa. Countries making up the Sahel include Mali, Mauritania, Niger, Senegal, Sudan, Burkina Faso, Chad, the Gambia and Guinea-Bissau.

sankofa An Adinkra symbol meaning 'Return and get it', representing the importance of learning from the past and the wisdom of using past experiences to build the future.

Shoowa Peoples of the kingdom of Kuba, located in what is now the Democratic Republic of Congo.

shweshwe A fabric based on a block and discharge printing technique on indigo cloth which was developed by European textile manufacturers in the 18th and 19th centuries.

smelting Reducing the metal to liquid form in order to extract it from the ore.

Tifinagh A modern form of Berber script used by the Tuareg to write Tamasheq, their language.

Tonga Peoples who inhabit northwestern Zimbabwe and southern Zambia.

Tuareg Nomadic pastoralist Berber peoples who inhabit the Saharan regions of North and West Africa including Niger, Mali, Libya, Algeria and Burkina Faso.

upcycling The process of converting old or discarded materials into useful and beautiful items.

Yoruba Peoples living in Southwestern Nigeria and Southern Benin in West Africa.

Zulu Peoples of South Africa, said to be the largest ethnic group.

Map

Morocco
Tunisia
Western Sahara
Algeria
Libya
Egypt
Mauritania
Mali
Niger
Chad
Sudan
Eritrea
Cape Verde
Senegal
Gambia
Burkina Faso
Guinea Bissau
Guinea
Djibouti
Somalia
Sierra Leone
Côte d'Ivoire
Ghana
Benin
Nigeria
Cameroon
Central African Republic
South Sudan
Ethiopia
Liberia
Togo
São Tomé and Príncipe
Equatorial Guinea
Gabon
Republic of Congo
Democratic Republic of Congo
Uganda
Kenya
Rwanda
Burundi
Angola
Tanzania
Seychelles
Angola
Malawi
Comoros
Zambia
Mozambique
Madagascar
Mauritius
Namibia
Zimbabwe
Botswana
Réunion
Swaziland
South Africa
Lesotho

Pages 202–208: Shine
Shine, textiles: No. 1
Football Fan, Jackie So,
Julie Juu, Obama.
Heidi Chisholm.

Further Reading & Resources

Books

Arts, Joss. *Vlisco: Textiles for Africa*. Zwolle: Waanders Publishing, 2012 • Bacquart, Jean-Baptiste. *The Tribal Arts of Africa: Surveying Africa's Artistic Geography*. London and New York: Thames & Hudson, 1998 and 2002, pp. 9–10, 12–14 • Gillow, John. *African Textiles: Colour and Creativity Across a Continent*. London: Thames and Hudson Ltd and San Francisco: Chronicle Books, 2003 and 2009, pp. 9, 13, 19, 109, 147, 173, 175, 181, 190, 213 • Hess, Janet B. *Art and Architecture in Postcolonial Africa*. North Carolina: McFarland and Company, Inc., and London: McFarland, 2006 • Hudson, Julie, and Christopher Spring. *North African Textiles*. London: British Museum Press and Washington, D.C.: Smithsonian Institution Press, 1995 • Picton, John, and John Mack. *African Textiles*. Colorado: Westview Press Inc. and London: British Museum Publications, 1989 • Spring, Christopher. *African Textiles Today*. London: British Museum Press, 2012, pp. 32, 100, 102, 105, 132, 144, 157 • Stokes Sims, Lowery, and Leslie King-Hammond. *The Global Africa Project*, New York: Prestel Publishing, 2010, pp. 140, 193, 201, 218. • Vogel, Susan. *Africa Explores: 20th Century African Art*. New York: Center for African Art, 1991

Articles

'African LookBook', 2012. www.african-lookbook.myshopify.com/blogs/african-lookbook/7547854-ousmane-mbaye • Akinwumi, Tunde. K. 'The "African Print" Hoax. Machine Produced Textiles Jeopardise African Print Authenticity.' *Journal of Pan African Studies*, vol. 2, no. 5, July 2008. www.jpanafrican.com/docs/vol2no5/2.5_African_Print.pdf, pp. 179–92 • Atwood, Roger. 'African Art: Beyond the Masks', 2012. www.artnews.com/2012/09/17/beyond-the-masks/ • The Batik Guild. 'The Art of Batik', 1999. www.batikguild.org.uk • Berman, Kelly. 'Design Indaba: The Quiet Ambassador of African Design', 2014. www.designindaba.com/articles/interviews/quiet-ambassador-african-design • Bouisson, Michel. 'Rue Diallo', VIA (Valorization of Innovation in Furnishing) • Bradley, Simon. 'Swiss Archaeologist Digs Up West Africa's Past', 2007. www.swissinfo.ch/eng/archive/Swiss_archaeologist_digs_up_West_Africas_past.html?cid=5675736 • Cape Craft and Design Institute, newsletter, April 2009. Bishop Tarambawamwe Wires the Old and Whirls the New, p. 5 • Da Gama. 'History of Shweshwe.' www.dagama.co.za/index.php?option=com_content&view=article&id=102&Itemid=164 • Ft.com. 'Furniture Made in Africa. Built for the World', 2013. www.ft.com/cms/s/2/c676c2e8-cdfb-11e2-a13e-00144feab7de.html#slide13,2 • Golden Hinde. 'A History of Goldwork Embroidery', 2009. www.golden-hinde.co.uk/36/HistoryOfGoldWork.html • Hofverberg, Hanna. 'Dorze Weaving in Ethiopia: A Model of Education for Sustainable Development?', 2010. www.diva-portal.org/smash/get/diva2:424776/FULLTEXT01.pdf • Kasfir, Sidney. 'African Art and Authenticity: A Text with a Shadow.' *African Arts*, vol. 25, no. 2, pp. 40–53, 96–97. UCLA James S. Coleman African Studies Centre, April 1992 • Luxury Society. 'Luxury Brands & the Promise of Africa: Suzy Menkes' www.luxurysociety.com/articles/2012/09/luxury-brands-the-promise-of-africa-suzy-menkes • Picton, John, and Janet B. Hess (accessed 2014). 'African Art.' www.britannica.com/EBchecked/topic/757032/African-art • Rawsthorn, Alice. 'Design Gets More Diverse.' www.nytimes.com/2011/03/21/arts/21iht-DESIGN21.html?ref=alicerawsthorn&_r=0 • Samuel P. Harn Museum of Art. 'Between the Beads: Reading African Beadwork', exhibition, November 2008–December 2009. http://ufdc.ufl.edu/UF00091311/00001 • Selvedge digital edition, issue 17, Poetry in Motion, p. 41 • UNESCO. 'Bark Cloth Making in Uganda', 2005. www.unesco.org/culture/intangible-heritage/40afr_uk.htm; Bike Tours. www.ibike.org/africaguide/textile/index.htm • Young, Robb. 'Africa's Fabric is Dutch', 2012. www.nytimes.com/2012/11/15/fashion/15iht-ffabric15.html?pagewanted=all&_r=4&

Museums, Collectors and Organizations

Africa Design Award: www.africadesignaward.org • African Creative Economy Conference: www.africacreativeconference.com • Arterial Network: www.arterialnetwork.org • The British Museum. Room 25: Africa, The Sainsbury Galleries. • Clarke, Duncan, Adire African Textiles. www.adireafricantextiles.com • Creative Africa: www.creative-africa.org • Design Network Africa (DNA): www.designnetworkafrica.org • Maker Faire Africa: www.makerfaireafrica.com • The Metropolitan Museum of Art. www.metmuseum.org/toah/hd/aima/hd_aima.htm • Museum of African Design (MOAD): www.moadjhb.com • Raw Material Company: www.rawmaterialcompany.org • Reid, Bryony, 2005. African Metalworking. Pitt Rivers Museum, University of Oxford. www.prm.ox.ac.uk/metalworking.html

Talks, Media, Events

Adichie, Chimamanda Ngozi. 'The Danger of a Single Story.' TED Talks. www.ted.com/talks/chimamanda_adichie_the_danger_of_a_single_story?language=en • African Masters, 2013. Episode 2: Creations. The Africa Channel UK • International Herald Tribune's IHT Luxury Conference, 2012. 'The Promise of Africa, The Power of the Mediterranean.' www.inytconferences.com/luxury-2012.aspx • Willard Musarurwa speaking at Design Indaba, 2010. www.designindaba.com/video/stephen-burks-recycles-inspire

Index

A

Africa Craft Trust 32
Africa Design Award 13, 128
Ahiagble, Gilbert 10
Aid to Artisans 12, 78, 114
Aid to Artisans Ghana 106
Aïssa Dione Tissus 146–49;
147–49
Alliance Française, Zimbabwe 32
appliqué 18–19, 20, 168
Artecnica 78–79; *79*
Arterial Network 12
artisan/s 9–15, 17, 19, 25–26,
36, 52, 56, 61, 66, 68, 70, 72, 78,
80, 86, 90, 96, 98, 102, 106, 113,
122, 124, 126, 128, 134, 136, 138,
141–42, 174, 194
Artlantique 62–65; *62–65*
aso oke 160; *111*
Association des Designers
Africains (African Designers
Association) 72
Attia, Hussein 136
Awosile, Yemi 200–201; *200–201*

B

bark cloth 18–19, 200–201, 141;
200–201
basketry 16, 25–41, 56, 130,
basket-making 56, 82, 128
basket-weavers 12, 32,
basket-weaving 12, 16, 25, 32,
36, 38, 82, 128
batik 20, 164, 166
beads 16, 19, 40, 113, 120, 126,
136
beading 18–19, 120; *4–5*
Benin 10, 162
Besbes, Mariem 15, 172–75;
173–75
Binga Craft Centre 30, 118
Birsel, Ayse 12, 66
Birsel + Seck 66–69; *3, 66–69*
bògòlanfini (mud cloth) 18,
141–42, 168, 171; *19, 144, 169,
170–71*
Boontje, Tord 12
Botswana 12, 19, 154–55
British Council, the 118, 200
Bulawayo Home Industries 30
Burkina Faso 13, 19, 74, 86–89,
148
Burks, Stephen 12, 78–79; *79*

C

Cameroon 164–67
Cape Craft and Design Institute
78, 120
carpentry 62, 80, 90
Central Africa 10, 17–20, 80
Centro de Arte Africana 114–15;
115
ceramics 9, 10, 16–17, 19, 25,
43–59, 126, 134
clay 14, 16–17, 43–46, 52, 56,
125–26
pottery 10, 52, 56, 194
Chahbar, Yasmina 136, 138
Chisholm, Heidi 186, 188
classical
classical African furniture 94
classical art 80, 96, 106
classical craft 12, 14–15, 106,
136
classical design 9, 136, 184
classical style 25
classical techniques 96
classical textiles 156
classical weaving cultures 148
classical weaving techniques
141
cotton, 18, 21, 148, 156, 178, 184,
190, 194–95
organic cotton 144, 148, 168,
196
craft(s) 13–15, 18, 20, 25–26, 30,
32, 38, 40–41, 43, 48, 78, 82, 96,
106, 113–14, 116, 122, 128, 136,
176, 178, 180, 182; *15*
craft development 32, 40
craft heritage 14, 26, 106, 128
craft skills 30
craft techniques 12, 30
craftsmanship 10–12, 14, 52,
80, 113, 134, 156, 160, 168
craftwork 10, 14–15, 30
hand-crafted 14, 30, 44, 49, 64,
80, 106, 114, 126, 128, 136
hand-craftsmanship 136, 154,
Crafts Council 200

D

decor 20, 38, 106, 120, 126, 146,
160
decorative objects 90, 114, 156
Da Gama 21; *21*
Dar Leone 156–57; *2, 156–57*

Davies Okundaye, Nike 10
Democratic Republic of Congo
19, 158–59
design 6–7, 9–11, 14–15, 25–26,
38, 40, 44, 50
Africa's design 7, 11, 14, 70
contemporary design 15, 25,
38, 44, 96, 116, 170, 184
design and creativity 7
design development 11–14, 68
design education 14
design industry 7, 9, 10–12, 70
design-led 12, 30, 32, 38
Design Indaba 40
Design Maketo 158–59; *159*
Design Museum, London 50
Design Network Africa (DNA) 9,
11–13, 46, 56, 74, 89, 98, 106, 118,
168, 180, 184; *8, 53–55, 57–59,
86–89, 99–101, 170–71, 185*
Diallo, Cheick 11–12, 70, 72, 106
Diallo Design 70–73; *1, 71– 73*
Diallo, Hamidou 194
digital printing 141, 156, 158, 164
Dione, Aïssa 15, 144, 146–48
Dlamini, Thembi 36
Dokter and Misses 74–77; *75–77*
Dole, Sandrine 12
Doumbia, Boubacar 168, 170–71
Dowuona, Joseph Nii Noi 52
Duplessis, Aïda 196, 198
du Toit, Philippa 126
du Toit, Werner 126
Dyalvane, Majolandile 44–46
dyes 18, 25, 36, 148, 168, 184
dyeing 18, 19, 36, 114, 154,
164, 166, 172, 194
indigo dyeing 142, 144, 194
natural dyes 168, 171–72, 180,
184
resist-dyeing 18, 166
synthetic dyes 18, 184
vegetable dye 18, 20, 148, 168,
172, 174, 194

E

East Africa 10, 18–21
eco-friendly 38, 180
Egypt 136–39
embroidery 18–20, 154
metal-thread embroidery 20
environmentally conscious 11, 116
environmental issues 150
Ercol 158–59

ethics 11–12
ethical awareness and
sustainability 196
Ethiopia 16, 18, 20, 32, 94–95,
141, 184–85
Everling, Edwin 30
exhibitions 12–13, 19, 30, 32, 40,
50, 66, 68, 72, 90, 105, 106, 118,
132, 158

F

Fabrica 40, 48
fairtrade 12, 38
Feeling African 78–79; *79*
felt, feltmaking 141, 180, 182
fibres 90, 142, 148, 172, 184, 194,
196, 198, 201
natural fibres 16, 19, 201
organic fibres 16, 19, 196
sustainable fibre 19
vegetable fibre 141, 148
Fick-Jordaan, Marisa 40–41
Fofana, Aboubakar 14–15,
142–45, 148; *143–45*
Folawiyo, Jade 48–50
Forson, Josephine 106–107
Forson, Kweku 106–107
France 70–73, 90–93, 154–55,
164–67, 194–95, 196–99
Freemantle, Sheila 36
Fulani 176–78
Funna, Isatu 156
furniture 61–111, 126, 136, 146,
150, 158, 160, 194

G

Galerie Arte 80–81; *80–81*
Geels, Abke 30
Germany 96–97, 160, 200
Ghana 20, 32, 52–55, 106–107,
162
Gillow, John 18
Guinea 142, 194–95

H

Habitat, UK 171
Haldane Martin 15, 82–85; *60–61,
82–85*
Hamed Design 9, 86–89; *8, 86–89*
handmade 10, 38, 80–81, 122,
126, 135, 144, 156, 176–78, 180,
182, 184

hand-weaving 146, 178, 196
hand-woven 30, 36, 78, 144, 146, 174, 176, 184, 194–95, 201
Haralambidou, Maria 12, 128
Heath Nash 113, 116–19; *112–13, 117–19*
heritage and culture 10–11, 106, 134
  artistic culture 30, 106
  culture 7, 10–12, 14–16, 18–19, 48, 70, 84, 86, 107, 109, 120, 134, 150, 154, 156, 160, 164, 178, 186
  heritage 7, 10–11, 15, 94, 114, 136, 184, 156, 170, 172
Hermès 146, 174
Hess, Janet B. 9, 18
Hlatswako, Siphiwe 36
Hoets, Adam 130
Hugo, Adriaan 74

I

identity 7, 11, 13, 82, 160, 176
  cross-cultural identity 43
  identity through design 116
Ilori, Yinka 108–11; *109–11*
Imiso Ceramics 43, 44–47; *42–43, 44–47*
India's National Institute of Design 25, 32–33; *24–25, 33–35*
indigo 18, 21, 30–31, 142, 144
  indigo *shweshwe* 21; *21*
  natural indigo 18, 141–42, 148, 194–95; *143–45*
industrial design 12–13, 74, 78, 82, 94
  industrial manufacturing 61, 130
interior design 66, 74, 82, 90, 105, 156
Islamic patterns 25, 130, 132
Côte d'Ivoire 18, 90–93, 134–35, 156

J

Jade Folawiyo 48–51; *49–51*
Johnson, Patty 12
Jomo Design Furniture 94–95; *95*
Jordaan, Ronél 56, 180–82

K

kanga cloth (*leso*) 20–21; *21*
Kasfir, Sidney Littlefield 10
Kasobané Group 168
Kassena people of Burkina Faso 74
Kebede, Henock 94
Kenya 21
Khmissa 96–97; *96–97*
Kitengela Glass, Kenya 188
Kouamo, Julie 164–67; *164–67*
Kpando 52–55, 72; *53–55*
Kuku, Banke 150–53; *150–53*
kuba cloth 19, 156; *19*

L

Lahlou, Hicham 13
Lamghari el Kossori, Bettina 96–97
Lamghari el Kossori, Said 96
laser cutting 74, 130
Le Bussy, Joëlle 14, 80–81
Le Ndomo 168–71; *169–71*
Liberia 18, 134
Li Edelkoort Studio 174
lighting 50, 116–19, 126–27, 130–33, 136–39
lighting and decor 113–39, 201
Llonch, Ramón 62–64
looms 18, 146
  contemporary, modern looms 146, 168
  hand-operated looms 18
  traditional looms 144, 176, 184, 194
  tree looms 176
Lupane Women's Centre 32–33; *33*

M

Mabeo Furniture 12
Mabeo, Peter 12
Mabuza, Ester 36
Madagascar 18, 26–29
Madwa 26–29; *26–29*
Maketo, Henoc 158–59
Makinen, Tuulia 194
Malawi 12, 20, 32, 128–29
Mali 18, 70–73, 142–45, 148, 168–71, 196–99
Mandjaque 146
Marshall, Kathy 184

Martin, Haldane 15, 82–85; *60–61, 82–85*
Martin-Leke, Swaady 134
Master Wire and Beadcraft 120–121; *121*
materials 8, 11, 15–17, 38, 48–49, 61, 70, 89, 90, 92, 96, 98, 105, 116, 126, 134, 136, 141, 148, 196, 200
  discarded fishing boats 62
  discarded materials 11, 61–62, 70, 80, 89, 96, 102, 108, 113, 116, 128
  discarded waste 116
  modern materials 25
  natural materials 98, 113, 148, 180
  organic materials 134
  reclaimed materials 11
  recyclable materials 25
  recycled materials 106
  salvaged materials 70, 96, 98
  sustainable materials 26
Mauritania 18, 141, 176–79
Mbaye, Ousmane 11, 102–103, 105
McGowan, Julian 12
McGowan, Trevyn 11, 12
Meeuwsen, Cecile 30
metal 9, 16–17, 19, 25, 30, 48, 50, 61, 70, 89, 102, 105, 106, 113–14
  gold 17, 20, 96–97, 122, 124, 134, 156
  hammered metal 17
  precious metals 113, 124
  scrap, discarded metal 70, 89, 102
  silver 17, 30–31, 96–97, 122, 124, 138
metalwork 16–17, 138
Michou 122, 124–25
Michou Bowls 122–25; *122–25*
Mngometulu, Elizabeth 36
Mondlane, Carlos 114–15
Moore, Heather 190
Morocco 11, 18, 96–97
Moroso, M'Afrique collection 66, 68
Moroso, Patrizia 7, 12, 68
Mozambique 18, 114–15
M'Rithaa, Mugendi K. 11, 15
mud cloth see *bògòlanfini*
Mud Studio 126–27; *1, 127*
Musarurwa, Willard 12, 78–79
Museum of African Design 13
Museum of Arts and Design, New

York 13, 40
Mutapo 56–59, 118; *57–59*
Mutuba Project, The 200–201

N

Nala family 10, 43
Namibia 19
Nash, Heath 11, 116
National Association of Craftsmen, Mozambique 144
National Institute of the Arts 31–33
nature 17, 44, 82, 98, 120, 126, 130, 134, 160, 164, 180, 196
Ndebele patterns 74
Netherlands, The 20, 30–31, 136–39, 154–55
Network of African Designers 12
New Basket Workshop, The 25, 32–35; *24–25, 33–35*
Niang, Babacar Mbodj 98
Niger 30–31
Nigeria 20, 48–51, 108–11, 150–53, 160–63, 200–201
North Africa 16–18, 20, 122, 124–25
Nulangee Design 98–101; *99–101*

O

Ouattara, Hamed 11, 86, 89
Ousmane Mbaye Design 102–105; *102–105*

P

patinization 50
People of the Sun 12, 128–29; *129*
Petel 176–79; *176–79*
Picasso, Pablo 14, 46
Picton, John 9
post-consumer waste 11, 116, 200
Poswa, Zizipho 44, 46
Potter, Frances 32
printed textiles 141, 150, 158
  screen-printing 158, 164, 166
product design 26, 32, 48, 50, 90, 108, 114
production 17, 38, 106, 114–15
  adapted production techniques 20
  contemporary production 43

environmentally conscious production 11–12
mass production 14, 138
natural production processes 141
production process 14, 36, 46, 68, 80, 86, 126
traditional production methods 82
traditional techniques 14, 30, 38, 48, 70, 141–42, 164, 166, 168

R

raffia 16, 19, 20, 148
recycling 9, 11, 12, 80, 102, 105, 106, 113, 116, 126, 128, 181
  recycled plastic 68, 82, 116; *5*
resourcefulness 10–11, 102
Roberts, Garth 12
Ronél Jordaan Textiles 180–83; *1, 57, 180–83*
Rushmere, Tracy 186, 188

S

Sabahar 184–85; *185*
Seck, Bibi 12, 13, 66
Sene, Baay Xaaly 10
Senegal 11, 17–18, 62–65, 66–69, 80–81, 98–101, 102–105, 146–49
Servais Somain, Jean 90–93; *91–93*
Shine Shine 186–89, 205; *186–89, 202–208*
shweshwe 21; *21*
Sierra Leone 18, 156–57
silk 18, 20
  Eri silk 184
silk-weaving 172
Sims, Lowery Stokes 13
sisal 25–26, 36
Sithole, Clive 43
Sithole, Nic 43
Skinny laMinx 190–93; *190–93*
social issues 11–12, 150
  social responsibility 12
Somian, Jean Servais 90, 92
Sonaike, Eva 160–63
Southbank Centre, London 200
Southern Africa 17–19, 118, 124–25
Southern Guild 46

South Africa 11, 13–14, 21, 26–29, 32–35, 38–41, 44–47, 74–77, 78–79, 82–85, 116–19, 120–21, 122–25, 126–27, 130–33, 134–35, 180–83, 186–89, 190–93
Spain 62–65
Spring, Christopher 18
Sserunkuuma, Bruno 43
STEP Trust's Honde Valley bamboo weavers 32–33; *33–35*
storytelling 154, 186
  Nigerian parables 108–11
sustainability 11, 13, 61, 66, 196
  sustainable approach to doing business 136
  sustainable business 144, 184
  sustainable craft 26, 114
  sustainable design 12–13, 108
  sustainable development 12, 128
  sustainable industry 11
Swaziland 26–29, 36–37

T

Tanzania 21
Taplin, Katy 74
Tarambawamwe, Bishop 120
Tariku, Jomo 94–95
Tate 200
Tavie 30–31; *31*
TEDGlobal 7
  TEDGlobal Africa Conference, Tanzania 40
Tekura 72, 106–107; *1, 107*
Tensira 194–95; *195*
textiles 9–10, 16, 18, 19, 20–21, 26, 46, 136, 141–201
  natural textiles 142
  textile design 62, 142, 150
  traditional textiles 154, 168, 178, 196; *15*
Tintsaba 36–37; *36–37*
Togo 148
Tunisia 18, 172–75

U

Uganda 18–19, 200–201
UNESCO 19, 174, 200
United Kingdom 48–51, 108–11, 150–53, 156–57, 158–59, 160–63, 164–67, 200–201
upcycling 11, 108
Urquiola, Patricia 12

USA 66–69, 94–95, 156–57, 176–79

V

van Mil, Bonana 154–55; *154–55*
Victoria & Albert Museum, London 200
visual art 9–11, 16
Vlisco 20; *21*
Vogel, Susan 9

W

Waddell, Inca 26
Waddell, Kathy 26
Wagne, Ibrahima 176
Wagne, Julie 176, 178
Wallace, Marjorie 56, 58, 118
water-gilding 122, 124
wax cloth 18, 20–21, 160; *21, 109, 111*
weaving 15–16, 18–19, 25–26, 30, 38, 85, 96, 141, 146, 148, 154, 160, 168, 172, 176, 178, 182, 184, 194, 196
  strip-weaving 18–19, 156, 168; *19*
  weavers 18, 25–26, 32–33, 36, 38, 70, 148, 160, 176, 178, 184, 196
West Africa 10, 12, 18, 19, 64, 90, 146, 156, 160, 162, 176, 194
Willems, Karin 136, 138
willowlamp 25, 130–33; *22–23, 131–33*
wire 12, 38, 40, 78, 85, 116
  galvanized steel wire 78, 116
  recycled stainless steel 82
  telephone wire 25, 38, 40, 120
  wire artist 78, 120
wood 17, 19, 61–63, 80–81, 90, 94, 96, 98, 100, 106, 108, 113, 122, 124
woodcarving 16–17, 64, 90, 94, 106, 114, 122, 124, 128; *16–17*
wool 172
  merino wool 180
  wool gauze 172, 174
World Fair Trade Organization 184

Y

Yéleen Design 196–99; *197–99*
YSWARA 134–35; *135*

Z

Zambia 32
Zangira, Basil 56
Zangira, Jairos 56
Zata, Abel 10
Zenza 136–39; *137–39*
ZENZULU™ 7, 38–41; *1, 6, 38–41*
Zienzele Foundation 32; *24–25*
Zimbabwe 18, 19, 32–35, 56–59, 78–79, 120–21, 154
Zochita Zambiri Enterprise 128

Picture Credits

Acknowledgments

'It takes a village to raise a child.' As in the words of this ancient African proverb, it has truly taken a global village to create this book. From London to Cape Town, Dakar to Melbourne, the creation of a book like this has required the input of many, and I am truly grateful to everyone who has given generously of their time and talents: to the designers and makers who agreed to take part, for making time in their busy schedules to share their stories with me – not forgetting all who work for them behind the scenes, from assistants to PR. Also to the often nameless artisans, whose unrivalled skills are vital to the development of Africa's design industries. To Jamie Camplin, Ilona de Nemethy

Sanigar and to all at Thames & Hudson who had a hand in bringing this from a dream to reality. To Mugendi K. M'Rithaa, Trevyn McGowan and the Design Network Africa Team, Fraser Conlon, David Ross, Duncan Clarke, Christopher Spring, and so many others who helped with information, image sourcing and advice.

To my Mum and Dad, for your love and support. To Faro and Tino, my dream team, for your encouragement. To Keisha and Kiana, and to family and friends, who kept me going whether they realized it or not! And above all, in everything I do, I give You thanks.